The Gospel According to Luke

Part One

Luke 1:1–11:54

Michael F. Patella

with Little Rock Scripture Study staff

Little Rock
Scripture Study

A ministry of the Diocese of Little Rock
in partnership with Liturgical Press

Nihil obstat for the commentary text by Michael F. Patella: Robert C. Harren, *Censor deputatus.*
Imprimatur for the commentary text by Michael F. Patella: ✠ John F. Kinney, Bishop of St. Cloud, Minnesota, August 30, 2005.

Cover design by Ann Blattner. Interior art by Ned Bustard.

 This symbol indicates material that was created by Little Rock Scripture Study to supplement the biblical text and commentary. Some of these inserts first appeared in the *Little Rock Catholic Study Bible*; others were created specifically for this book by Clifford M. Yeary.

1   2   3   4   5   6   7   8   9

Library of Congress Control Number: 2018946232
ISBN 978-0-8146-6368-4   ISBN 978-0-8146-6393-6 (e-book)

Office of the Bishop

DIOCESE OF LITTLE ROCK

2500 North Tyler Street • P.O. Box 7565 • Little Rock, Arkansas 72217 • (501) 664-0340 Fax (501) 664-6304

Dear Friends,

The Bible is a gift of God to the church, the people gathered around the world throughout the ages in the name of Christ. God uses this sacred writing to continue to speak to us in all times and places.

I encourage you to make it your own by dedicated prayer and study with others and on your own. Little Rock Scripture Study is a ministry of the Catholic Diocese of Little Rock. It provides the tools you need to faithfully understand what you are reading, to appreciate its meaning for you and for our world, and to guide you in a way that will deepen your own ability to respond to God's call.

It is my hope that the Word of God will empower you as Christians to live a life worthy of your call as a child of God.

Sincerely in Christ,

✠ Anthony B. Taylor
Bishop of Little Rock

TABLE OF CONTENTS

Wrap-up lectures are available for each lesson at no charge. The link to these free lectures is LittleRockScripture.org/Lectures/LukePartOne.

Welcome

The Bible is at the heart of what it means to be a Christian. It is the Spirit-inspired word of God for us. It reveals to us the God who created, redeemed, and guides us still. It speaks to us personally and as a church. It forms the basis of our public liturgical life and our private prayer lives. It urges us to live worthily and justly, to love tenderly and wholeheartedly, and to be a part of building God's kingdom here on earth.

Though it was written a long time ago, in the context of a very different culture, the Bible is no relic of the past. Catholic biblical scholarship is among the best in the world, and in our time and place, we have unprecedented access to it. By making use of solid scholarship, we can discover much about the ancient culture and religious practices that shaped those who wrote the various books of the Bible. With these insights, and by praying with the words of Scripture, we allow the words and images to shape us as disciples. By sharing our journey of faithful listening to God's word with others, we have the opportunity to be stretched in our understanding and to form communities of love and learning. Ultimately, studying and praying with God's word deepens our relationship with Christ.

The Gospel of Luke, Part One
Luke 1:1–11:54

The resource you hold in your hands is divided into six lessons. Each lesson involves personal prayer and study using this book *and* the experience of group prayer, discussion, and wrap-up lecture.

If you are using this resource in the context of a small group, we suggest that you meet six times, discussing one lesson per meeting. Allow about 90 minutes for the small group gathering. Small groups function best with eight to twelve people to ensure good group dynamics and allow all to participate as they wish.

WHAT MATERIALS WILL YOU USE?

The materials in this book include:

- The text of the Gospel of Luke, chapters 1:1–11:54, using the New American Bible, Revised Edition as the translation.

- Commentary by Michael F. Patella (which has also been published separately as part of the New Collegeville Bible Commentary series).
- Occasional inserts ◉ highlighting elements of the chapters of Luke being studied. Some of these appear also in the *Little Rock Catholic Study Bible* while others are supplied by staff writers.
- Questions for study, reflection, and discussion at the end of each lesson.
- Opening and closing prayers for each lesson, as well as other prayer forms available in the closing pages of the book.

In addition, there are wrap-up lectures available for each lesson. Your group may choose to purchase a DVD containing these lectures or make use of the audio or video lectures online at no charge. The link to these free lectures is: LittleRockScripture.org/Lectures/LukePartOne. Of course, if your group has access to qualified speakers, you may choose to have live presentations.

Each person will need a current translation of the Bible. We recommend the *Little Rock Catholic Study Bible*, which makes use of the New American Bible, Revised Edition. Other translations, such as the New Jerusalem Bible or the New Revised Standard Version: Catholic Edition, would also work well.

HOW WILL YOU USE THESE MATERIALS?

Prepare in advance

Using Lesson One as an example:

- Begin with a simple prayer like the one found on page 11.
- Read the assigned material in the printed book for Lesson One (pages 12–18) so that you are prepared for the weekly small group session. You may do this assignment by reading a portion over a period of several days (effective and manageable) or by preparing all at once (more challenging).
- Answer the questions, Exploring Lesson One, found at the end of the assigned reading, pages 19–21.
- Use the closing prayer when you complete your study. This prayer may be used again when you meet with the group.

Meet with your small group

- After introductions and greetings, allow time for prayer (about 5 minutes) as you begin the group session. You may use the prayer found on page 11 (also used by individuals in their preparation) or use a prayer of your choosing.

- Spend about 45–50 minutes discussing the responses to the questions that were prepared in advance. You may also develop your discussion further by responding to questions and interests that arise during the discussion and faith-sharing itself.

- Close the discussion and faith-sharing with prayer, about 5–10 minutes. You may use the closing prayer at the end of each lesson or one of your choosing at the end of the book. It's important to allow people to pray for personal and community needs and to give thanks for how God is moving in your lives.

- Listen to or view the wrap-up lecture associated with each lesson (15–20 minutes). You may watch the lecture online, use a DVD, or provide a live lecture by a qualified local speaker. This lecture provides a common focus for the group and reinforces insights from each lesson. You may view the lecture together at the end of the session or, if your group runs out of time, you may invite group members to watch the lecture on their own time after the discussion.

Above all, be aware that the Holy Spirit is moving within and among you.

The Gospel According to
Luke

Part One

LESSON ONE

Introduction and Luke 1

Begin your personal study and group discussion with a simple and sincere prayer such as:

Prayer

O God of Joy, send your Spirit with a freshness that will help me hear familiar words with open ears and heart. Guide me as I pray and study the Gospel of Luke.

Read the introduction to Luke on pages 12–13 and the Bible text of Luke 1 found in the outside columns of pages 14–18, highlighting what stands out to you.

Read the accompanying commentary to add to your understanding.

Respond to the questions on pages 19–21, Exploring Lesson One.

The closing prayer on page 21 is for your personal use and may be used at the end of group discussion.

INTRODUCTION

The Gospel of Luke, the third Gospel in the New Testament canon, has a remarkable place in the study of Sacred Scripture, and this unique position does not stem solely from the fact that it is the only Gospel to have a second volume associated with it, namely, the Acts of the Apostles. Luke engenders a great deal of discussion on the level of New Testament formation, sensitivity to historical data, literary technique, and theological development. This commentary deals with these areas to a greater or lesser degree.

The Gospel message

Each Gospel relates a particular evangelist's theological interpretation of the kerygma, that is, the passion, death, and resurrection of Jesus. To do this, the Gospel writer takes events from Jesus' life as passed down from traditions and sources and composes a Gospel account. Under the inspiration of the Holy Spirit, an evangelist uses his composition to present his particular theology of redemption mediated through Christ's life. Details may or may not be accurate, but the truth of the Gospel goes beyond details. The central focus of this study, therefore, is the theological picture that Luke's Gospel paints of Jesus, his earthly ministry, and the early church.

Matthew, Mark, Luke, and John

Anyone reading the Gospels notices that there are stories within them that overlap, parallel, and seemingly copy each other. The reason for, and explanation of, this problem have been part of the church since the beginning. Scholars such as Origen and Augustine were among the first to develop theories on the formation of the Gospels. In the modern era, new theories have arisen that have continued the dialogue and discussion on the development of the New Testament.

The brevity of this commentary prevents any lengthy discussion of the sources Luke used in writing his Gospel; this question has an involved and complicated history. For simplicity's sake, our commentary notes the names of commonly held sources as well as the familiar vocabulary of biblical scholarship. Knowing the following terms will be most helpful:

- *Canon:* the official collection of books comprising the Bible.

- *Codex Sinaiticus* and *Codex Vaticanus:* two of the most dependable, extant New Testament manuscripts.

- *Eschaton:* the final times bringing God's eternal plan to fulfillment. The study and interpretation of the eschaton is called eschatology.

- *Evangelist:* the name given to the four Gospel writers: Matthew, Mark, Luke, and John.

- *Kerygma:* the proclamation of the passion, death, and resurrection of Christ that also describes how salvation comes through participation in the same passion, death, and resurrection.

- *Parallel:* a term used to describe a passage in one Gospel that has a like passage in another Gospel.

- *Q:* a hypothetical, oral source that contains material common to Matthew and Luke but not Mark.

- *Synoptics:* the Gospels of Matthew, Mark, and Luke, so named because they share so much of the same narrative line as well as the same material.

- *Textual witness:* early written documents containing all or part of the biblical canon.

Luke the evangelist

Not much is known about the evangelist Luke. The tradition says that he was both a physician and an artist from Syria who completed his Gospel between A.D. 80 and 90. Using Acts 20–28 as a guide, along with Colossians 4:14 and Philemon 1:24, many feel that he may have known Paul. Although it is impossible to prove these claims, the texts that Luke wrote indicate that he was a highly educated person, influential in the early church, aware of geography (outside Palestine anyway) and history, and very much attuned to the dynamic, direction, and development of Christianity.

Sensitivity to historical data

In addition to being considered a doctor and an artist, many have thought of Luke as a historian, because he gives greater attention to historical details than any other evangelist. For example, passages describing the birth of Jesus and the ministry of John the Baptist contain information on emperors, governors, and kings, and a good deal of it is close to accurate. Much of our information about Pontius Pilate comes from Luke. In large part, his information about the Herodian dynasty matches well with the writings of the ancient Jewish historian Flavius Josephus.

Literary technique

Luke is an economical writer. This evangelist avoids repetitions and superfluous information. He tells a story well, with attention given to rising action, climax, and denouement. His use of Greek is among the finest in the New Testament, and he is well-versed in Greco-Roman literary style. His prose has a nobility that has made this Gospel a favorite of many.

Theological development

Luke views the passion, death, and resurrection of Christ as the great salvific act that has affected the whole cosmos. The evangelist expresses this theology by presenting Jesus' earthly ministry as a battle between Christ and Satan. Christ's victory over evil comes with his death and resurrection. In Lukan theology, the death on the cross is actually a transfiguration into glory. Furthermore, by virtue of that death, the same transformative glory is promised to humanity, a concept that came to be known as *theosis*.

In this presentation, Luke relies on literary motifs to relay these key concepts. First, there is the motif of the diabolical force. Every good story needs an antagonist, and Luke elevates Satan to this position. Consequently, Christ's miracles and cures are more than kind deeds; they are attacks against the Evil One and his diabolical force. In other words, Christ is in a relentless pursuit of redeeming the world from Satan's clutches.

Second is the idea of the great reversal, a term used to describe the turn in fortune that will befall all between now and the eschaton, that is, the end times: the hungry now will have a banquet, while the rich go hungry; the humble will be exalted, and the exalted will be humbled.

Next, there is the schism motif. Christ will come to all, but some will heed his call to discipleship while others will not.

Finally, there is joy. The word appears more times in the third Gospel than in any other New Testament work. In Lukan theology, for a world redeemed and transfigured by the blood of Christ, there can be no other Christian response than joy.

I: The Prologue

CHAPTER 1

¹Since many have undertaken to compile a narrative of the events that have been fulfilled among us, ²just as those who were eyewitnesses from the beginning and ministers of the word have handed them down to us, ³I too have decided, after investigating everything accurately anew, to write it down in an orderly sequence for you, most excellent Theophilus, ⁴so that you may realize the certainty of the teachings you have received.

continue

THE PROLOGUE

Luke 1:1-4

1:1-4 Address to Theophilus

The Gospel opens with a short prologue of a single periodic sentence, a style typical of ancient literature that often sets the tone and purpose of biographies and histories. Josephus and Polybius, for example, show similar introductions. Luke's use of this style often raises the question of whether he sees himself as writing a biography or a history. Opinions favoring one or the other abound. Perhaps the most we can say is that Luke is simply following the literary convention of the day as he writes his two-volume work. The Gospel, neither a biography nor a history, is an evangelical proclamation. A Gentile audience would expect such a prologue, and Luke is simply supplying it.

The identity of Theophilus is unknown. Possibilities range from his being a benefactor of the community, a church leader, or even a civil authority. Perhaps Theophilus is all three. On the other hand, using the name Theophilus (literally, "Beloved of God") universalizes the identity and allows every reader to be the addressee.

The prologue provides hints at the formation of the New Testament as well as the development of the early Christian community.

What are the "events that have been fulfilled"? Who are the "eyewitnesses" and "ministers of the word"? Luke describes some of these events and personages within his two-volume work, particularly in the Acts of the Apostles, but how much of it is recoverable is difficult to answer. Of fascinating interest for source critics is Luke's explanation that he has investigated "everything accurately anew, to write it down in an orderly sequence." How many and varied were the initial documents before they saw their final editing at Luke's hand? Extant papyri, lectionaries, and targums certainly bespeak a Christian movement very much in ferment and development. Luke's project replaced the diverse gospel fragments floating around the Greco-Roman world. That this Gospel eventually became part of the New Testament canon attests to its nearly universal use over the course of the first two centuries.

THE INFANCY NARRATIVE

Luke 1:5–2:52

Only Matthew and Luke feature stories of the birth of Christ, although from two different perspectives. Luke centers his account on Mary, while Matthew focuses on Joseph. It is obvious that Matthew and Luke were not copying each other in forming their respective infancy narratives. Nonetheless, they do share some details. Both have an angel relaying the divine plan to the human participants—Joseph in Matthew, Mary in Luke. Both state that this child will be born of the house of David in Bethlehem, that his name will be Jesus, and that these events will occur while Herod the Great is king of Judea (37 B.C.–4 B.C.). Most importantly, despite the many variations in the two different accounts, the two agree on the essential point that Mary is pregnant, and there is no human father.

Luke's purpose for including the infancy narratives is to situate the whole Gospel within the story of God's divine plan. Luke also uses references and allusions to the Old Testament, especially prophetic figures. Furthermore, he has passages dealing with John the Baptist precede those of Jesus. This structure prepares the reader for an account that aims to show Jesus as the one long-promised to deliver humankind from sin and death. Luke's infancy narratives grab the attention of his Gentile audience, catechize them, and graft them to the community of Israel by setting the many references to political events and leaders of the day within the context of the Old Testament. As Simeon proclaims in his canticle (2:29-32), Jesus is "a light for revelation to the Gentiles, / and glory for [the] people Israel" (2:32). Furthermore, this glory will not come easily, for even Jesus' mother, Mary, will be pierced by a sword. Thus, the infancy narratives serve as an abbreviated version of the Gospel and Acts. In the Acts of the Apostles, Luke recounts how Peter, Paul, and the Gentiles receive the light of revelation, but only after hardship and pain. On the final page of Acts, Paul is living, preaching, and teaching in that most Gentile of cities, Rome.

1:5-25 Announcement of the birth of John the Baptist

Luke provides a broad context for Jesus' birth, employing both Old Testament prophecies and typologies. Zechariah and Elizabeth are described as being "advanced in years," and thus past the age of childbearing. The an-

II: The Infancy Narrative

Announcement of the Birth of John

⁵In the days of Herod, King of Judea, there was a priest named Zechariah of the priestly division of Abijah; his wife was from the daughters of Aaron, and her name was Elizabeth. ⁶Both were righteous in the eyes of God, observing all the commandments and ordinances of the Lord blamelessly. ⁷But they had no child, because Elizabeth was barren and both were advanced in years. ⁸Once when he was serving as priest in his division's turn before God, ⁹according to the practice of the priestly service, he was chosen by lot to enter the sanctuary of the Lord to burn incense. ¹⁰Then, when the whole assembly of the people was praying outside at the hour of the incense offering, ¹¹the angel of the Lord appeared to him, standing at the right of the altar of incense. ¹²Zechariah was troubled by what he saw, and fear came upon him. ¹³But the angel said to him, "Do not be afraid, Zechariah, because your prayer has been heard. Your wife Elizabeth will bear you a son, and you shall name him John. ¹⁴And you will have joy and gladness, and many will rejoice at his birth, ¹⁵for he will be great in the sight of [the] Lord. He will drink neither wine nor strong drink. He will be filled with the holy Spirit even from his mother's womb, ¹⁶and he will turn many of the children of Israel to the Lord their God. ¹⁷He will go before him in the spirit and power of Elijah to turn the hearts of fathers toward children and the disobedient to the understanding of the righteous, to prepare a people fit for the Lord." ¹⁸Then Zechariah said to the angel, "How shall I know this? For I am an old man, and my wife is advanced in years." ¹⁹And the angel said to him in reply, "I am Gabriel, who stand before God. I was sent to speak to you and to announce to you this good news. ²⁰But now you will be speechless and unable to talk until the day these things take place, because you did not believe my words, which will be fulfilled at their proper time."

continue

²¹Meanwhile the people were waiting for Zechariah and were amazed that he stayed so long in the sanctuary. ²²But when he came out, he was unable to speak to them, and they realized that he had seen a vision in the sanctuary. He was gesturing to them but remained mute. ²³Then, when his days of ministry were completed, he went home. ²⁴After this time his wife Elizabeth conceived, and she went into seclusion for five months, saying, ²⁵"So has the Lord done for me at a time when he has seen fit to take away my disgrace before others."

Announcement of the Birth of Jesus

²⁶In the sixth month, the angel Gabriel was sent from God to a town of Galilee called Nazareth, ²⁷to a virgin betrothed to a man named Joseph, of the house of David, and the virgin's name was Mary. ²⁸And coming to her, he said, "Hail, favored one! The Lord is with you." ²⁹But she was greatly troubled at what was said and pondered what sort of greeting this might be. ³⁰Then the angel said to her, "Do not be afraid, Mary, for you have found favor with God. ³¹Behold, you will conceive in your womb and bear a son, and you shall name him Jesus. ³²He will be great and will be called Son of the Most High, and the Lord God will give him the throne of David his father, ³³and he will rule over the house of Jacob forever, and of his kingdom there will be no end." ³⁴But Mary said to the angel, "How can this be, since I have no relations with a man?" ³⁵And the angel said to her in reply, "The holy Spirit will come upon you, and the power of the Most High will overshadow you. Therefore the child to be born will be called holy, the Son of God. ³⁶And behold, Elizabeth, your relative, has also conceived a son in her old age, and this is the sixth month for her who was called barren; ³⁷for nothing will be impossible for God." ³⁸Mary said, "Behold, I am the handmaid of the Lord. May it be done to me according to your word." Then the angel departed from her.

continue

nouncement of the Baptist's birth, therefore, is similar to the miraculous birth genre found with Abraham and Sarah (Gen 18:1-15), Manoah and his wife (Judg 13:2-25), and Elkanah and Hannah (1 Sam 1:1-23). In addition, both Zechariah and Elizabeth are of priestly stock, which means that their son John would one day be serving in the temple at Jerusalem. None of the evangelists, however, imply that John the Baptist ever took on this role.

As a priest, Zechariah would take his turn serving in the temple twice a year for a week at a time. This detail no doubt led to the tradition, dating from at least the sixth century, that Ein Karem, with its close proximity to Jerusalem, is the village of John's birth.

Angels are God's messengers and agents, and Luke mentions them twenty-five times in the Gospel. More than half of these occurrences fall within the first two chapters. The presence of an angel at the altar of incense (v. 11) underscores God's role in the events to follow. While in Matthew's Gospel the angel who appears to Joseph (1:20) remains unnamed, Luke specifies the identity of the heavenly messenger who comes to both Zechariah and Mary. The name Gabriel itself is a combination of two Hebrew terms, *Gabur* ("strong man," "warrior"), and *El* ("God"), therefore "Warrior of God." Gabriel has a role in the Old Testament. In the book of Daniel, this angel explains a vision to Daniel (8:17-26) while simultaneously giving Daniel understanding (9:22).

1:26-45 Announcement of the birth of Jesus and Mary's pregnancy

In Luke's chronology, Gabriel's announcement to Zechariah (1:8-20) precedes the one to Mary (1:26-38). Luke is setting the proper sequence of salvation history. If John is the precursor of Jesus in the ministry, he must also come first in the order of birth. In the sixth month of Elizabeth's pregnancy, Gabriel comes to Nazareth to deliver the news to Mary. Of course, Mary is extremely puzzled by this information, and when she expresses her doubt (v. 29), Gabriel encourages her. When

Zechariah doubts, however, he is made mute (vv. 18, 20).

Whatever point Luke is trying to make by this comparison of the two personages, it is not too clear. Perhaps it is another way to indicate the Baptist's subservience to Christ, a point reiterated by the baby's leaping in Elizabeth's womb upon hearing Mary's greeting. Or since the recovery of Zechariah's voice excites wonder in the people (vv. 60-64), Zechariah's muteness reflects Luke's attention to the details of storytelling; it advances the theme and the plot.

The angel **Gabriel** is an Old Testament figure (Deut 8:16; 9:21-27) who is one of the heavenly messengers God uses to reveal special messages to human beings. In Daniel, his presence evokes terror; in this passage his message to Mary is likely interpreted as unsettling, although she accepts it with grace.

1:46-55 The Canticle of Mary

Traditionally called the *Magnificat* in the Western church where it is sung at Evening Prayer, the canticle has all the markings of an early hymn. There are four hymns in these opening narratives, of which this is the first. Grounded in a reference to Abraham and referencing other forebears, this song has a decidedly Jewish-Christian cast. The piece contains the reversal theme found in 1 Samuel 2:1-10, but it is modified. Those who oppress now will be overthrown, and the lowly will be exalted; those who are hungry now will have their fill, but those who are satiated now will be sent away.

The church uses the **Canticle of Mary** at Evening Prayer in the Liturgy of the Hours. It expresses a perfect model of surrender to God's will for every Christian, an attitude of surrender as the day begins to draw to a close.

Mary Visits Elizabeth

[39]During those days Mary set out and traveled to the hill country in haste to a town of Judah, [40]where she entered the house of Zechariah and greeted Elizabeth. [41]When Elizabeth heard Mary's greeting, the infant leaped in her womb, and Elizabeth, filled with the holy Spirit, [42]cried out in a loud voice and said, "Most blessed are you among women, and blessed is the fruit of your womb. [43]And how does this happen to me, that the mother of my Lord should come to me? [44]For at the moment the sound of your greeting reached my ears, the infant in my womb leaped for joy. [45]Blessed are you who believed that what was spoken to you by the Lord would be fulfilled."

The Canticle of Mary

[46]And Mary said:

"My soul proclaims the greatness of the Lord;
    [47]my spirit rejoices in God my savior.
[48]For he has looked upon his handmaid's
        lowliness;
    behold, from now on will all ages call me
        blessed.
[49]The Mighty One has done great things for
        me,
    and holy is his name.
[50]His mercy is from age to age
    to those who fear him.
[51]He has shown might with his arm,
    dispersed the arrogant of mind and heart.
[52]He has thrown down the rulers from their
        thrones
    but lifted up the lowly.
[53]The hungry he has filled with good things;
    the rich he has sent away empty.
[54]He has helped Israel his servant,
    remembering his mercy,
[55]according to his promise to our fathers,
    to Abraham and to his descendants for-
        ever."

[56]Mary remained with her about three months and then returned to her home.

continue

The Birth of John

⁵⁷When the time arrived for Elizabeth to have her child she gave birth to a son. ⁵⁸Her neighbors and relatives heard that the Lord had shown his great mercy toward her, and they rejoiced with her. ⁵⁹When they came on the eighth day to circumcise the child, they were going to call him Zechariah after his father, ⁶⁰but his mother said in reply, "No. He will be called John." ⁶¹But they answered her, "There is no one among your relatives who has this name." ⁶²So they made signs, asking his father what he wished him to be called. ⁶³He asked for a tablet and wrote, "John is his name," and all were amazed. ⁶⁴Immediately his mouth was opened, his tongue freed, and he spoke blessing God. ⁶⁵Then fear came upon all their neighbors, and all these matters were discussed throughout the hill country of Judea. ⁶⁶All who heard these things took them to heart, saying, "What, then, will this child be?" For surely the hand of the Lord was with him.

The Canticle of Zechariah

⁶⁷Then Zechariah his father, filled with the holy Spirit, prophesied, saying:

⁶⁸"Blessed be the Lord, the God of Israel,
    for he has visited and brought redemption to his people.
⁶⁹He has raised up a horn for our salvation
    within the house of David his servant,
⁷⁰even as he promised through the mouth of
    his holy prophets from of old:
⁷¹salvation from our enemies and from
    the hand of all who hate us,
⁷²to show mercy to our fathers
    and to be mindful of his holy covenant
⁷³and of the oath he swore to Abraham our
    father,
    and to grant us that,
⁷⁴rescued from the hand of enemies,
    without fear we might worship him
⁷⁵in holiness and righteousness
    before him all our days.

continue

⁷⁶And you, child, will be called prophet of
    the Most High,
    for you will go before the Lord to prepare
        his ways,
⁷⁷to give his people knowledge of salvation
    through the forgiveness of their sins,
⁷⁸because of the tender mercy of our God
    by which the daybreak from on high will
        visit us
⁷⁹to shine on those who sit in darkness and
    death's shadow,
    to guide our feet into the path of peace."

⁸⁰The child grew and became strong in spirit, and he was in the desert until the day of his manifestation to Israel.

1:57-80 The birth of John and the Canticle of Zechariah

Zechariah regains his speech upon acknowledging the divinely given name of his son. The hymn Zechariah sings, also known by its Latin name, the *Benedictus*, the Morning Prayer canticle in the Roman Office, clarifies John the Baptist's role in the sweep of salvation history. He is to "go before the Lord to prepare his ways" (v. 76). The beautiful, poetic images "daybreak from on high will visit us" (v. 78) and "to shine on those who sit in darkness and death's shadow" (v. 79) have their foundation in Isaiah 8:23–9:2. Luke concludes this section on John the Baptist with a brief note placing John in the desert, where the reader will encounter him again at the beginning of chapter 3. The evangelist now moves on to the birth of Christ.

The church uses the **Canticle of Zechariah** at Morning Prayer in the Liturgy of the Hours. It expresses God's awesome power to save all through Jesus Christ and is appropriate to beginning the day.

EXPLORING LESSON ONE

1. What are the four major motifs, or themes, found in the Gospel of Luke, as described in the Introduction to the commentary?

_____

_____

_____

_____

_____

_____

2. How and why did Luke go about writing his Gospel (1:1-4)? How might you be called to spread the Good News?

_____

_____

_____

_____

_____

_____

3. Who might Theophilus have been (1:3)? What are some of the possibilities?

_____

_____

_____

_____

_____

4. According to the angel, what will be John the Baptist's mission to Israel (1:15-17)?

_____

_____

_____

_____

_____

5. Matthew 1:18-25 and Luke 1:26-38 both have annunciation narratives. How do they differ from each other? What do they have in common?

_____

_____

_____

_____

_____

6. When has learning of someone's pregnancy made your heart leap with joy (1:39-45)?

_____

_____

_____

_____

_____

7. In the Canticle of Mary (1:46-55), in what verses do you see the theme identified as the great reversal?

_____

_____

_____

_____

_____

_____

8. a) Why did Elizabeth's neighbors and relatives object to having her son named John (1:57-61)?

_____

_____

_____

b) What triggers Zechariah's renewed ability to speak (1:62-64)?

_____

_____

_____

9. a) In the Canticle of Zechariah (1:67-79), what wonderful things does he foresee occurring through the one who will be "a horn for our salvation" (1:71-75)?

_____

_____

_____

b) What does Zechariah say will be John's role in God's plan of salvation (1:76-79)?

_____

_____

_____

CLOSING PRAYER

Prayer

"And how does this happen to me, that the mother of my Lord should come to me?"
(Luke 1:43)

Where are you present, Lord, in the world where we live? How will we recognize and acknowledge your coming? Teach us to open our eyes and look for you. Give us the wisdom to be in awe of your presence. We pray for the ministries in our parish that help to make your presence known, especially . . .

LESSON TWO

Luke 2

Begin your personal study and group discussion with a simple and sincere prayer such as:

Prayer

O God of Joy, send your Spirit with a freshness that will help me hear familiar words with open ears and heart. Guide me as I pray and study the Gospel of Luke.

Read the Bible text of Luke 2 found in the outside columns of pages 24–28, highlighting what stands out to you.

Read the accompanying commentary to add to your understanding.

Respond to the questions on pages 30–32, Exploring Lesson Two.

The closing prayer on page 32 is for your personal use and may be used at the end of group discussion.

CHAPTER 2

The Birth of Jesus

¹In those days a decree went out from Caesar Augustus that the whole world should be enrolled. ²This was the first enrollment, when Quirinius was governor of Syria. ³So all went to be enrolled, each to his own town. ⁴And Joseph too went up from Galilee from the town of Nazareth to Judea, to the city of David that is called Bethlehem, because he was of the house and family of David, ⁵to be enrolled with Mary, his betrothed, who was with child. ⁶While they were there, the time came for her to have her child, ⁷and she gave birth to her firstborn son. She wrapped him in swaddling clothes and laid him in a manger, because there was no room for them in the inn.

continue

2:1-7 The birth of Jesus

Scholars have often considered Luke's attention to historical detail as one indication of the evangelist's high level of education—not only for the fact that he includes such information but more for the way in which he uses it. Greco-Roman historians wrote their accounts to favor their patrons or the party in power, much the same way as a local chamber of commerce writes about its particular locale today. Thucydides, Tacitus, and Josephus all had a certain editorial slant to their works that supported those who supported them. Luke stands within this tradition, but with an important difference: his bias is toward showing the hand of the holy Spirit at work in both Jewish and Gentile events of the day. Jesus Christ is to be considered the fulfillment of both cultural worlds. We have observed an example of Jewish fulfillment in the stories of Zechariah, Elizabeth, and Mary. In these opening verses of chapter 2, we see the events in the pagan world also cooperating and foretelling the birth of the Messiah in Jesus Christ.

A difficulty enters into this section with the names and dates of the people mentioned. Although the Roman historian Suetonius states that there were registrations of Roman citizens in 28 B.C., 8 B.C., and A.D. 14 (*Divus Augustus* 27.5), there is no record, outside the New Testament, which states that Caesar Augustus (27 B.C.–A.D. 14) decreed the enrollment of the whole empire, that is, non-citizens, for taxation or any other purposes. There were local registrations within various provinces from time to time, and once such census occurred under the Roman legate Quirinius, but he was not made governor of Syria until A.D. 6, when he also took control of Judea at the banishment of Herod's son Archelaus. Since Luke attests that both John the Baptist and Jesus were born under Herod the Great (37 B.C.–4 B.C.), most scholars concur that it would be impossible for these events to have occurred at a time when Caesar Augustus, Herod the Great, and Quirinius were all simultaneously in power.

For Luke's theological intention, however, the important point is that during the *Pax Romana*, when the Gentile world looked to Augustus Caesar as the prince of peace, Jesus comes into the world as the true Prince of Peace. In fulfillment of the Old Testament prophecies, which establish the messianic line through the house of David, Jesus, a descendant of David, is born in Bethlehem, the city of David. In order to make this point, Luke takes historical facts, such as the census, and reworks them to fit his theological purpose, just as ancient historians altered details to suit the purposes of their patrons. For contemporary readers, such remolding of details may seem spurious or dishonest, but in the religious tradition, the truth that Jesus is the Savior of the world lies beyond the accuracy of some facts dealing with the reigns of various rulers.

The Greek term *phatnē* is translated as "manger" (v. 7) but can also mean "stable." The Greek *kataluma*, represented here as "inn," specifically means "lodging" or "guestroom," with space for a dining area (*kataluma* is the word employed in Luke 22:11). Reading together both *phatnē* and *kataluma*, we can see that Luke is probably describing the typical house of the day. These homes, built for extended families, had a living space on the upper floors with a stable at ground level. Both Matthew and Luke emphasize Jesus' Davidic lineage through his foster father, Joseph, as well as the fact that Jesus is born in Bethlehem, the city of David. It is reasonable to conclude that Joseph had family in Bethlehem and that he and Mary stayed with them. With all the relatives of the extended family eating and sleeping in the upper *kataluma*, the one private place for Mary to give birth would be in the *phatnē* or stable.

According to Roman, Greek, Coptic, Armenian, and other ancient traditions, the phrase "firstborn son" (v. 7) represents a title of honor. It does not imply that Mary had other children after Jesus.

2:8-20 Angels and shepherds

Once again Luke uses an angel to announce a birth, this time to the shepherds. Shepherds, although not social outcasts, were among the poorest people in the society. A group composed mostly of women and young children, they did not own land or sheep, and they worked for hire. Luke underscores Jesus' salvific role especially for the poor with this annunciation story; the shepherds are the first to hear the good news. With the angelic choir

---

⁸Now there were shepherds in that region living in the fields and keeping the night watch over their flock. ⁹The angel of the Lord appeared to them and the glory of the Lord shone around them, and they were struck with great fear. ¹⁰The angel said to them, "Do not be afraid; for behold, I proclaim to you good news of great joy that will be for all the people. ¹¹For today in the city of David a savior has been born for you who is Messiah and Lord. ¹²And this will be a sign for you: you will find an infant wrapped in swaddling clothes and lying in a manger." ¹³And suddenly there was a multitude of the heavenly host with the angel, praising God and saying:

¹⁴"Glory to God in the highest
    and on earth peace to those on whom his
    favor rests."

continue

(v. 14) we have the third song in the infancy narratives, the *Gloria*. In Western liturgies this text serves as the foundation for the "Glory to God."

2:21-38 Circumcision, naming, and presentation in the temple

The parallel between John the Baptist and Jesus continues in verse 21. John is circumcised and named eight days after his birth (1:59-60), and now so too with Jesus.

In portraying this section, Luke relies on some elements of the Mosaic Law as well as stories about the prophet Samuel (1 Sam 1:24-28). God commands Abraham to circumcise male descendants and slaves as a sign of the covenant (Gen 17:12), a point the book of Leviticus stipulates (12:3). Although Luke states that both parents must undergo the rites of purification (v. 22), the Levitical prescriptions apply only to the mother (Lev 12:2-5). A Gentile Christian himself, Luke is not always accurate in his explanation of Jewish cultic and legal codes. Luke rightly notes that the firstborn must be consecrated to the Lord (Exod

The Visit of the Shepherds

¹⁵When the angels went away from them to heaven, the shepherds said to one another, "Let us go, then, to Bethlehem to see this thing that has taken place, which the Lord has made known to us." ¹⁶So they went in haste and found Mary and Joseph, and the infant lying in the manger. ¹⁷When they saw this, they made known the message that had been told them about this child. ¹⁸All who heard it were amazed by what had been told them by the shepherds. ¹⁹And Mary kept all these things, reflecting on them in her heart. ²⁰Then the shepherds returned, glorifying and praising God for all they had heard and seen, just as it had been told to them.

The Circumcision and Naming of Jesus

²¹When eight days were completed for his circumcision, he was named Jesus, the name given him by the angel before he was conceived in the womb.

The Presentation in the Temple

²²When the days were completed for their purification according to the law of Moses, they took him up to Jerusalem to present him to the Lord, ²³just as it is written in the law of the Lord, "Every male that opens the womb shall be consecrated to the Lord," ²⁴and to offer the sacrifice of "a pair of turtledoves or two young pigeons," in accordance with the dictate in the law of the Lord.

²⁵Now there was a man in Jerusalem whose name was Simeon. This man was righteous and devout, awaiting the consolation of Israel, and the

continue

Nothing else is known about the identities of Simeon and Anna other than what this section tells us. Both represent the faithful Israelite who waits and does not lose hope in the coming redemption. Simeon's canticle, or *Nunc dimitiis* (2:29-32), is the fourth and final hymn from the Lukan infancy narratives and has traditionally been part of Compline or night office in the Liturgy of the Hours.

Simeon's words to Mary, ominous though they are, are also highly theological. With verse 34 we see the first instance of the schism motif, which runs throughout Luke's Gospel. Often in Luke's portrayal of Jesus' mission, one party or person will follow him, while another will turn away. One group will be saved, another will fall into perdition. In each case individuals choose their own fate by deciding for or against following Jesus. Simeon states that a sword will pierce Mary's heart as well. The discipleship that Jesus demands extends even to his mother. Not only does Luke indicate through Simeon that discipleship will not be easy, but he also elevates Mary to the role of the model disciple. To love Jesus is to suffer with him.

The widowed state of the prophetess Anna, daughter of Phanuel (vv. 36-38), has made her utterly dependent on God's goodness. Luke tells us that she "spoke about the child to all who were awaiting the redemption of Jerusalem" (v. 38), and thus she is the first evangelist. By starting out with the "redemption of Jerusalem," Luke sets his literary project in order. After the resurrection, the message goes from "Jerusalem, throughout Judea and Samaria, and to the ends of the earth" (Acts 1:8).

Simeon and Anna and the Value in Waiting

If you have ever been promised something for which you had to wait a very long time, you might be able to appreciate the tenacity of Simeon and Anna. Schooled in the faithfulness of God throughout the history of their people, they anticipated God's action in some profound way.

13:2), but this redemption is accomplished by paying five shekels to a priest (Num 3:47-48). The sacrifice of turtledoves Luke describes is part of a woman's purification rite. These verses serve to emphasize Mary and Joseph as faithful, law-abiding Jews, and with them, Luke underscores the Jewish context of Jesus' birth and mission.

It is not just their waiting that leads them to recognize that the child Jesus is the beginning of promises fulfilled. It is what they did with their waiting. Simeon is a man of prayer who experiences the Spirit and finds in the temple the sign he has been told to expect. Anna is a prophetess, in the long tradition of Israel's prophets, who reads the signs of the times and speaks for God. She spends her time at the temple in prayer and fasting.

Both Simeon and Anna illustrate that waiting involves action and contemplative listening. They go to the place where their faith finds its home and they are people of prayer. They were not simply in the right place at the right time; they were in the right space spiritually and recognized the time of God's action.

2:39-40 Nazareth and Bethlehem

According to the accounts of both Luke and Matthew, Jesus is born in Bethlehem but spends his youth and young adulthood in Nazareth. Mention of these two locales in this manner forms an enigmatic knot that is difficult to unravel. If there are serious questions surrounding the census (see 2:1-7 above), why do Mary and Joseph go to Bethlehem, when we know that Mary is from Nazareth (1:26)? The four Gospels and the Acts of the Apostles refer to "Jesus of Nazareth" but never "Jesus of Bethlehem." Is the whole narrative of the birth at Bethlehem a literary construction serving to demonstrate that Jesus, through his foster father Joseph, is the Son of David who is born in the city of David?

Scripture, history, and archaeology all show that there was a strong Jewish presence in various parts of Galilee, so it would not be a strange place for Jesus to have his upbringing. The most we can say about this puzzlement is that the two sources that mention Jesus' birth, Luke and Matthew, both specifically state that it occurs in Bethlehem. There are no texts that

holy Spirit was upon him. [26]It had been revealed to him by the holy Spirit that he should not see death before he had seen the Messiah of the Lord. [27]He came in the Spirit into the temple; and when the parents brought in the child Jesus to perform the custom of the law in regard to him, [28]he took him into his arms and blessed God, saying:

> [29]"Now, Master, you may let your servant go
> in peace, according to your word,
> [30]for my eyes have seen your salvation,
> [31]which you prepared in sight of all the
> peoples,
> [32]a light for revelation to the Gentiles,
> and glory for your people Israel."

[33]The child's father and mother were amazed at what was said about him; [34]and Simeon blessed them and said to Mary his mother, "Behold, this child is destined for the fall and rise of many in Israel, and to be a sign that will be contradicted [35](and you yourself a sword will pierce) so that the thoughts of many hearts may be revealed." [36]There was also a prophetess, Anna, the daughter of Phanuel, of the tribe of Asher. She was advanced in years, having lived seven years with her husband after her marriage, [37]and then as a widow until she was eighty-four. She never left the temple, but worshiped night and day with fasting and prayer. [38]And coming forward at that very time, she gave thanks to God and spoke about the child to all who were awaiting the redemption of Jerusalem.

The Return to Nazareth

[39]When they had fulfilled all the prescriptions of the law of the Lord, they returned to Galilee, to their own town of Nazareth. [40]The child grew and became strong, filled with wisdom; and the favor of God was upon him.

continue

cite Nazareth as Jesus' birthplace. Basing their respective accounts on the oral tradition, the evangelists composed stories that get Mary

The Boy Jesus in the Temple

[41]Each year his parents went to Jerusalem for the feast of Passover, [42]and when he was twelve years old, they went up according to festival custom. [43]After they had completed its days, as they were returning, the boy Jesus remained behind in Jerusalem, but his parents did not know it. [44]Thinking that he was in the caravan, they journeyed for a day and looked for him among their relatives and acquaintances, [45]but not finding him, they returned to Jerusalem to look for him. [46]After three days they found him in the temple, sitting in the midst of the teachers, listening to them and asking them questions, [47]and all who heard him were astounded at his understanding and his answers. [48]When his parents saw him, they were astonished, and his mother said to him, "Son, why have you done this to us? Your father and I have been looking for you with great anxiety." [49]And he said to them, "Why were you looking for me? Did you not know that I must be in my Father's house?" [50]But they did not understand what he said to them. [51]He went down with them and came to Nazareth, and was obedient to them; and his mother kept all these things in her heart. [52]And Jesus advanced [in] wisdom and age and favor before God and man.

and Joseph to Bethlehem and then back up to Nazareth. The importance of this Lukan narrative is that Jesus stands in line of the Davidic Messiah, and about that, Luke wants the reader to know, there can be no doubt.

2:41-52 The boy Jesus in the temple

Only Luke contains this story of how Jesus is lost while on the return trip from Jerusalem. Passover was one of the pilgrimage feasts, when devout Jews would go to Jerusalem to celebrate the occasion.

The story itself reflects a theological point that Luke makes explicit in recounting Jesus' earthly ministry: true discipleship goes beyond familial relationships (8:19-21 and 11:27-29). In addition, that this conversation takes place in the temple reflects Luke's ambivalent attitude toward the temple's existence, if not his positive disposition toward it. Luke frequently shows Jesus teaching in the temple up to the final days before his crucifixion. In the Acts of the Apostles, Peter and Paul also preach and teach in the temple.

Jesus returns with his parents to Nazareth, and nothing more is heard about him until he is an adult and begins his ministry. The next time we read of Jesus in Jerusalem will be at his triumphal entry (19:28-39), which leads to his death.

Mary, Mother of Jesus

Surprisingly, the New Testament records very little about the details of Mary's background and life. The primary focus is on her relationship to her son Jesus. That her parents were named Joachim and Anna comes from a later apocryphal gospel (Protoevangelium of James, second century AD). We do not know when she was born or under what circumstances, but the church honors her above all other women for being the mother of Jesus, God's only begotten Son. Whereas the gospels hint that she was from a poor family in Nazareth, the apocryphal story asserts that she was born of wealthy parents in Jerusalem who served in the temple.

Of the gospels, Luke gives the most attention to Mary. Artists throughout history have portrayed poignant scenes from Luke's infancy narrative (chaps. 1–2) such as the annunciation and the visitation. Mary takes center stage throughout the story as it unfolds and her destiny to be the mother of Jesus is revealed. Mary expresses her response to God's mysterious will in the Canticle of Mary (Luke 1:46-55). Filled with Old Testament imagery, it shows that Mary acquiesces totally to God's will, even without understanding it fully.

All of the gospels feature Mary in some fashion, but John never names her. He refers to her only as "the mother of Jesus." Yet she figures prominently in John at the foot of the cross, where she becomes an icon of the church, entrusted to the care of the unnamed Beloved Disciple (John 19:26-27).

Matthew's story of Jesus' miraculous conception (chaps. 1–2) emphasizes Joseph's role as the foster father of Jesus, whose Davidic lineage confirms that Jesus is the fulfillment of messianic expectations. In Matthew, Mary is seen primarily in a subservient role, humbly accepting God's will, guided and protected by her betrothed's actions.

Mark does not include an infancy narrative, but Mary is located among Jesus' relatives. Jesus is called "son of Mary" (Mark 6:3), but she herself may be numbered among those relatives who think, because of his unusual ministry, he is "out of his mind" (Mark 3:21)!

Acts portrays Mary as a member of the early Christian community (1:14), but Paul makes almost no reference to her, except through the acknowledgment that Jesus was "born of a woman" (Gal 4:4).

The church's understanding of Mary's significance grew over time, beyond the testimony of the Bible, under the guidance of the Holy Spirit, and expressed through official church teachings. Most important, the church honors Mary for her role in salvation history. By saying "yes" to God's mysterious will, she enabled salvation to enter the world through the birth of her son.

The Roman Catholic Church has bestowed on Mary many honorific titles (Mother of God, Mother of the Church, the New Eve, Queen of Heaven, Star of the Sea, etc.) and has also proclaimed doctrines about her immaculate conception (1854) and assumption into heaven (1950). She is also identified with the unnamed woman "clothed with the sun" of the book of Revelation (12:1-18), an uncertain but ancient interpretation. After the Second Vatican Council, ecumenical dialogues promoted discussion among Roman Catholics and Protestants about Mary's significance, which led to a proliferation of books on Mary.

EXPLORING LESSON TWO

1. What problems are created for modern historians by the details Luke provides concerning the date of Jesus' birth (2:1-3)?

_____

_____

_____

_____

2. a) Joseph and Mary travel from Nazareth to Bethlehem when Mary is far along in her pregnancy (2:1-5). When has it seemed that a serious inconvenience revealed God working in some way in your life?

_____

_____

_____

   b) Why is it important for Jesus to be born in Bethlehem? (See 1 Sam 17:12; Mic 5:1; Matt 2:1-6.)

_____

_____

_____

3. In Luke's account of Jesus' birth (2:6-14), where do you see some of Luke's concern for the poor?

_____

_____

_____

_____

4. The shepherds faithfully reported the good news of Jesus' birth (2:15-18). How have you grown into an awareness of the significance of Jesus' birth, and who have you shared that good news with?

_____

_____

_____

_____

_____

5. What elements of Luke's account of the nativity (Luke 1–2) are you most likely to keep for reflection in your heart (2:18-19)?

_____

_____

_____

_____

_____

_____

6. What is the story behind your first (or baptismal) name? How or why was that name chosen (2:21)?

_____

_____

_____

_____

_____

_____

7. What might "the consolation of Israel" have meant to Simeon (2:25-32)? (See Isa 40:1-2; 42:6-7; 46:13; 49:6; 52:9-10.)

_____

_____

_____

_____

_____

8. What important virtues do you see Simeon and Anna demonstrating (2:25-38)?

_____

_____

_____

_____

_____

_____

9. In what ways was Jesus' childhood similar to that of any good but normal boy (2:40-52)? How was he also exceptional?

_____

_____

_____

_____

_____

10. How do you imagine Mary and Joseph dealt with each other and their own emotions while they searched for Jesus (2:41-45)? How do you imagine their prayer during their search?

_____

_____

_____

_____

_____

CLOSING PRAYER

Prayer

[Anna] gave thanks to God and spoke about the child to all who were awaiting the redemption of Jerusalem.   (Luke 2:38)

Give us, Jesus, the zeal and faithfulness of Anna who spoke of you to all she met. May our experiences of you send us forth as faith-filled witnesses of your saving power. We pray now in thanksgiving for these people who have given witness to us, especially . . .

LESSON THREE

Luke 3–5

Begin your personal study and group discussion with a simple and sincere prayer such as:

Prayer

O God of Joy, send your Spirit with a freshness that will help me hear familiar words with open ears and heart. Guide me as I pray and study the Gospel of Luke.

Read the Bible text of Luke 3–5, found in the outside columns of pages 34–46, highlighting what stands out to you.

Read the accompanying commentary to add to your understanding.

Respond to the questions on pages 47–49, Exploring Lesson Three.

The closing prayer on page 50 is for your personal use and may be used at the end of group discussion.

III: The Preparation for the Public Ministry

CHAPTER 3

The Preaching of John the Baptist

¹In the fifteenth year of the reign of Tiberius Caesar, when Pontius Pilate was governor of Judea, and Herod was tetrarch of Galilee, and his brother Philip tetrarch of the region of Ituraea and Trachonitis, and Lysanias was tetrarch of Abilene, ²during the high priesthood of Annas and Caiaphas, the word of God came to John the son of Zechariah in the desert. ³He went throughout [the] whole region of the Jordan, proclaiming a baptism of repentance for the forgiveness of sins, ⁴as it is written in the book of the words of the prophet Isaiah:

"A voice of one crying out in the desert:
'Prepare the way of the Lord,
    make straight his paths.
⁵Every valley shall be filled
    and every mountain and hill shall be
        made low.
The winding roads shall be made straight,
    and the rough ways made smooth,
⁶and all flesh shall see the salvation of God.' "

⁷He said to the crowds who came out to be baptized by him, "You brood of vipers! Who warned you to flee from the coming wrath? ⁸Produce good fruits as evidence of your repentance; and do not begin to say to yourselves, 'We have Abraham as our father,' for I tell you, God can raise up children to Abraham from these stones. ⁹Even now the ax lies at the root of the trees. Therefore every tree that does not produce good fruit will be cut down and thrown into the fire."

¹⁰And the crowds asked him, "What then should we do?" ¹¹He said to them in reply, "Whoever has two tunics should share with the person who has none. And whoever has food should do likewise." ¹²Even tax collectors came to be baptized and they said to him, "Teacher, what should we do?" ¹³He answered them, "Stop collecting

continue

THE PREPARATION FOR THE PUBLIC MINISTRY

Luke 3:1–4:13

John the Baptist is the precursor of Jesus, and Luke shifts the focus from one ministry to the other. This transition entails Jesus' baptism and desert temptation.

3:1-20 The ministry of John the Baptist

Chapter 3, like chapter 1, opens with a periodic sentence, a strong indication that this section is a major literary unit.

As with the birth of Jesus (Luke 2:1-3), Luke situates John the Baptist within a geopolitical framework involving the Roman emperor and his Palestinian-Jewish client states. Tiberius Caesar succeeds Augustus. According to Luke's dating, the word of God comes to the desert-dwelling John the Baptist in A.D. 29.

The nominally Jewish king, Herod the Great, died in 4 B.C. and divided his kingdom among his three sons: Herod Antipas, the tetrarch, or ruler, of Galilee and Perea; Herod Archelaus, ethnarch over Judea, Idumea, and Samaria; and Herod Philip, the tetrarch in charge of Gaulanitis, Trachonitis, and Batanaea. Archelaus's misrule led the emperor Augustus to banish him in A.D. 6, at which time a Roman procurator was appointed to govern his territory. One such procurator was Pontius Pilate, who ruled the area from A.D. 26 to 36, the period Luke is writing about here.

Lysanias is difficult to identify. There is scant information about a person of that name ruling the area of Abilene at this time. Many have speculated on the reason why Luke includes this information. Was he addressing a Christian community based in Abilene (northwest of Damascus), or was he from Abilene himself? We may never know, but we have here a typical example of the manner in which Luke uses historical data—truth is more important than mere fact.

With the mention of high priests, Annas and Caiaphas, Luke grounds the Baptist's ministry within the history of Jewish Palestine. From John's Gospel (11:49; 18:13), we read that Caiaphas is the priest at the time of Jesus' death. Although only one high priest ruled at a time, Luke may include the reference to Annas simply because Annas was still alive while his son Caiaphas was in charge.

John the Baptist begins the public ministry in the parallel accounts of the other three Gospels as well, but just where John preaches is a question. Mark simply says "in the desert" (1:4). Matthew states "in the desert of Judea" (3:1), which would place him under the jurisdiction of Pontius Pilate. Further on, both Matthew and Mark add that crowds come from Judea and Jerusalem, a region accessible to Perea and Herod Antipas's territory. Luke writes "in the desert . . . [the] whole region of the Jordan" (vv. 2-3), a reading that suggests along the Jordan River, including the Judean side of the river (Roman territory), but in any case, in that area east of Jerusalem as far as the mountains on the east bank. Since Galilee is also under Herod Antipas, Luke seems to introduce the idea that both Jesus and John, each in his proper time, face the same political ruler (see 3:19ff. and 23:6-12).

Luke firmly establishes John as the precursor. Not only does John preach a baptism of repentance for the forgiveness of sins, but the evangelist (vv. 4-6) also interprets the Baptist's role as the fulfillment of Isaiah's prophecy (40:3-5).

Judaism, with its whole tradition of the mikvah, or ritual bath, was well acquainted with the water ablutions that John mentions (v. 16). The reference to a baptism "with the holy Spirit and fire" further on in the verse

more than what is prescribed." [14]Soldiers also asked him, "And what is it that we should do?" He told them, "Do not practice extortion, do not falsely accuse anyone, and be satisfied with your wages."

[15]Now the people were filled with expectation, and all were asking in their hearts whether John might be the Messiah. [16]John answered them all, saying, "I am baptizing you with water, but one mightier than I is coming. I am not worthy to loosen the thongs of his sandals. He will baptize you with the holy Spirit and fire. [17]His winnowing fan is in his hand to clear his threshing floor and to gather the wheat into his barn, but the chaff he will burn with unquenchable fire." [18]Exhorting them in many other ways, he preached good news to the people. [19]Now Herod the tetrarch, who had been censured by him because of Herodias, his brother's wife, and because of all the evil deeds Herod had committed, [20]added still another to these by [also] putting John in prison.

The Baptism of Jesus

[21]After all the people had been baptized and Jesus also had been baptized and was praying, heaven was opened [22]and the holy Spirit de-

continue

emphasizes that Jesus' action goes beyond religious ritual; it will have an efficacy that will transform the whole created order, just as fire alters the material state of matter. Early Christian mosaics depict this point by presenting Jesus standing in the Jordan River with smiling fish surrounding his feet as the Baptist pours water over Jesus' head.

3:21-22 The baptism of Jesus

John clarifies his subservient role to Christ with his preaching in 3:15-18. From the beginning of Luke's Gospel, information about John the Baptist has come before the accounts dealing with Jesus. In keeping with this thematic development of the Baptist as precursor, Luke scended upon him in bodily form like a dove. And a voice came from heaven, "You are my beloved Son; with you I am well pleased."

The Genealogy of Jesus

²³When Jesus began his ministry he was about thirty years of age. He was the son, as was thought, of Joseph, the son of Heli, ²⁴the son of Matthat, the son of Levi, the son of Melchi, the son of Jannai, the son of Joseph, ²⁵the son of Mattathias, the son of Amos, the son of Nahum, the son of Esli, the son of Naggai, ²⁶the son of Maath, the son of Mattathias, the son of Semein, the son of Josech, the son of Joda, ²⁷the son of Joanan, the son of Rhesa, the son of Zerubbabel, the son of Shealtiel, the son of Neri, ²⁸the son of Melchi, the son of Addi, the son of Cosam, the son of Elmadam, the son of Er, ²⁹the son of Joshua, the son of Eliezer, the son of Jorim, the son of Matthat, the son of Levi, ³⁰the son of Simeon, the son of Judah, the son of Joseph, the son of Jonam, the son of Eliakim, ³¹the son of Melea, the son of Menna, the son of Mattatha, the son of Nathan, the son of David, ³²the son of Jesse, the son of Obed, the son of Boaz, the son of Sala, the son of Nahshon, ³³the son of Amminadab, the son of Admin, the son of Arni, the son of Hezron, the son of Perez, the son of Judah, ³⁴the son of Jacob, the son of Isaac, the son of Abraham, the son of Terah, the son of Nahor, ³⁵the son of Serug, the son of Reu, the son of Peleg, the son of Eber, the son of Shelah, ³⁶the son of Cainan, the son of Arphaxad, the son of Shem, the son of Noah, the son of Lamech, ³⁷the son of Methuselah, the son of Enoch, the son of Jared, the son of Mahalaleel, the son of Cainan, ³⁸the son of Enos, the son of Seth, the son of Adam, the son of God.

continue

skillfully provides the account of John's arrest (3:19-20) before the narrative surrounding Jesus' baptism (3:21-22).

Luke shows Jesus praying at critical points in his life. To underscore the point that John is lesser than Jesus, Luke recounts the baptism itself in the passive voice. There is no conversation between the two individuals. Jesus is baptized as one among the crowd, the voice from heaven is directed only to him, and it is understood that the others do not hear it. Later, when the Baptist sends messengers to Jesus (7:18-23), there is no indication of his being aware of having baptized Jesus.

To interpret the baptism, Luke relies on a conflation of two Old Testament passages. The first half of the voice from heaven (v. 22) is a paraphrase of Psalm 2:7, while the second half is part of Isaiah 42:1. It should be noted, however, that the textual witnesses for this section display a wide variety of readings. One manuscript, for example, quotes Psalm 2:7 in its entirety: "You are my Son; today I have begotten you." The version that we have here reflects the evidence from Codices Vaticanus and Sinaiticus, two of the most dependable of the extant Gospel manuscripts. A similar, although not an exact, quotation is found at the transfiguration of Jesus (9:35).

According to the science of the ancients, doves were considered not to have any bile and thus were symbolic of virtue. Not only were they worthy for sacrifice to God, but, as seen here, they also symbolized the divine presence.

3:23-38 The genealogy of Jesus

By setting Jesus' genealogy after the baptism, Luke fashions a twofold theological statement. First, after having seen Jesus' divine sonship pronounced in the voice from heaven (3:22), he now reiterates that point by stating it in verse 38. Second, Luke writes Jesus' ancestral line going all the way back to Adam, and by so doing connects Jesus to all humanity, unlike Matthew, who shows Jesus as descended from Abraham to stress his Jewish background and role (Matt 1:1-17). Luke also underscores Jesus' virginal conception by the use of the parenthetical expression "as was thought" (v. 23).

One theory of the formation of Luke's Gospel holds that the infancy narratives (Luke 1–2) were later additions to a primitive version of the current text (see above). If so, an earlier stage of the Third Gospel began with Jesus' baptism and genealogy. Supporting this possibility is a lack of similar introductory material in the other Gospels (Matthew notwithstanding), as well as use of Luke's Gospel by early Christians and heretics, particularly Marcion, who denied Christ's relationship with anyone in the Old Testament. In any case, in this final redaction Luke does a fine job linking the first two chapters to the third both literarily and theologically.

4:1-13 The temptation in the desert

The Spirit who descended upon Jesus at his baptism now leads him into the desert for forty days.

CHAPTER 4

The Temptation of Jesus

[1]Filled with the holy Spirit, Jesus returned from the Jordan and was led by the Spirit into the desert [2]for forty days, to be tempted by the devil. He ate nothing during those days, and when they were over he was hungry. [3]The devil said to him, "If you are the Son of God, command this stone to become bread." [4]Jesus answered him, "It is written, 'One does not live by bread alone.'" [5]Then he took him up and showed him all the kingdoms of the world in a single instant. [6]The devil said to

continue

 Both Luke and Matthew include genealogies in their infancy narratives. They vary in ways that likely reveal the theological interests of each evangelist, respectively.

Matthew's Genealogy (1:1-17)	Luke's Genealogy (3:23-38)
Placed at the beginning of the Gospel; alludes to a new "beginning" of salvation history in Jesus out of Israel's history	Placed between Jesus' baptism and temptation by the devil to emphasize Jesus as God's Son
Begins with Abraham, father of faith, and then structured in rough chronological order around three groups of fourteen kings each, with David as the central figure, emphasizing Jesus' Davidic heritage and the fulfillment of the Abrahamic covenant of becoming a "father of many nations"	Structured in reverse chronological order around significant figures (not kings) in Israel's history and concluding with Adam, "son of God," emphasizing the universalism of salvation achieved in Jesus, savior of all humankind
Interjects four female figures in the list (Tamar, Rahab, Ruth, the wife of Uriah the Hittite), perhaps emphasizing God's ability to write salvation history in extraordinary ways (all bore sons in unusual circumstances), thus prefiguring Mary's role as the bearer of Jesus, Emmanuel	Absence of women
Heightened role of Joseph in the infancy narrative as foster father and protector of Jesus	Heightened role of Mary in the infancy narrative as hearer and doer of God's word

him, "I shall give to you all this power and their glory; for it has been handed over to me, and I may give it to whomever I wish. ⁷All this will be yours, if you worship me." ⁸Jesus said to him in reply, "It is written:

'You shall worship the Lord, your God,
and him alone shall you serve.'"

⁹Then he led him to Jerusalem, made him stand on the parapet of the temple, and said to him, "If you are the Son of God, throw yourself down from here, ¹⁰for it is written:

'He will command his angels concerning
you,
to guard you,'

¹¹and:

'With their hands they will support you,
lest you dash your foot against a stone.'"

¹²Jesus said to him in reply, "It also says, 'You shall not put the Lord, your God, to the test.'" ¹³When the devil had finished every temptation, he departed from him for a time.

continue

The desert brings life right to the edge. In the Jewish tradition, it can be a place of divine encounter, such as with Moses and the burning bush (Exod 3:1-14), or it can be the place of death (see Gen 21:14-16). Of course, the forty-year wandering of the Israelites, a communal experience that formed them into the people of God, takes place in the desert. Just so, Jesus' sojourn in the wilderness brings into clearer focus for him what his mission on earth will be.

The Synoptic Gospels all include the desert temptation, but there are differences among them in the telling. Mark's account is the shortest (1:12-13), and Luke's is most similar to Matthew's (4:1-11), but the similarities break down in the respective nuances of each account. In Matthew, the setting of the three temptations goes from the desert, to Jerusalem, to the kingdoms of the world, while in Luke we read desert, kingdoms of the world, Jerusalem. Luke's account has greater internal consistency, for Jesus' ministry will culminate in Jerusalem, and it will be in that city that he meets his greatest temptation as well as his greatest triumph (see below, Luke 22:39-46; 23:44-49; 24). As it stands in this passage, the three temptations are to riches, glory, and power, represented by bread, rule, and defiance of nature respectively. Jesus' reply to each of the temptations, all from the book of Deuteronomy (8:3; 6:13, 16), connects his experience in the desert with that of the wandering Israelites.

For Luke, the devil is a force in the yet unredeemed world of Jesus' ministry. In the Lukan narrative, this encounter in the desert is Jesus' first meeting with the devil, but certainly not the last (v. 13). Jesus will be in hard combat with the devil or Satan from here until his death.

THE MINISTRY IN GALILEE

Luke 4:14–9:50

The Spirit now leads Jesus to Galilee, the area north of Jerusalem and Samaria. This was the district of his upbringing, and he begins his earthly ministry there.

4:14-30 Jesus arrives in Nazareth

From the preceding section we know that Jesus was away from the region and his hometown. What is unclear, however, is how long he was away and why he departed. That he was baptized with all the people somewhere along the Jordan (3:3, 21) has led many to conclude that Jesus was associated with John the Baptist for some time before setting out on his own way.

Jesus reads from Isaiah 61:1-2, a messianic text. Although by the fourth century A.D. the rabbis had adopted a particular order of scriptural pericopes to be read throughout the year, it is uncertain whether such a system was in place in first-century Judaism. If it was, then Jesus demonstrates his authority in bypassing the accepted practice and choosing a passage of his own. His concluding comment (v. 21) allows the listeners to draw their own conclusions.

The reaction of the people in Nazareth reflects the schism motif, which Luke develops from the beginning (see 2:34). Some speak highly of Jesus, while others are filled with resentment at having one of their own preach to them, and Jesus calls them on this point by providing examples from their history when the people acted in like manner. The references to Elijah and Elisha serve to describe the kind of prophet people see in Jesus and, indeed, how he perhaps sees himself. Unlike the prophets of the south, such as Isaiah and Jeremiah, Elijah and Elisha lived in the north, and they, too, made the rounds raising the dead, feeding the poor, and healing the sick (1 Kgs 17:1–2 Kgs 13). Since Galilee is in the north, where much of Jesus' ministry is situated, both the actions and words of Jesus would have special resonance with the people. Jesus' comments draw the obvious conclusion. By their resistance to him, the townspeople are no better than their forebears who did not heed earlier prophets; therefore, they come under the same judgment. Jesus' insinuation enrages the people to the point where they try to kill him.

Nazareth is located on a hill overlooking the Esdraelon Plain. A rocky precipice encircles the southeast section of the town.

4:31-44 Exorcisms, cures, and healings at Capernaum

The central focus of Jesus' ministry is the reclamation of this world for the reign of God, and now the battle begins.

Capernaum lies along the northern shore of the Sea of Galilee, where archaeological evidence points to its being a busy fishing village. Much of Jesus' ministry takes place in this locale.

Unlike the temptation scene in Luke 4:1-13, here Jesus encounters not the devil but an unclean demon. For Luke, both the demon and the devil may represent the same evil force, but they are not one and the same entities. The

IV: The Ministry in Galilee

The Beginning of the Galilean Ministry

[14]Jesus returned to Galilee in the power of the Spirit, and news of him spread throughout the whole region. [15]He taught in their synagogues and was praised by all.

The Rejection at Nazareth

[16]He came to Nazareth, where he had grown up, and went according to his custom into the synagogue on the sabbath day. He stood up to read [17]and was handed a scroll of the prophet Isaiah. He unrolled the scroll and found the passage where it was written:

[18]"The Spirit of the Lord is upon me,
    because he has anointed me
        to bring glad tidings to the poor.
He has sent me to proclaim liberty to captives
        and recovery of sight to the blind,
            to let the oppressed go free,
[19]and to proclaim a year acceptable to the Lord."

[20]Rolling up the scroll, he handed it back to the attendant and sat down, and the eyes of all in the synagogue looked intently at him. [21]He said to them, "Today this scripture passage is fulfilled in your hearing." [22]And all spoke highly of him and were amazed at the gracious words that came from his mouth. They also asked, "Isn't this the son of Joseph?" [23]He said to them, "Surely you will quote me this proverb, 'Physician, cure yourself,' and say, 'Do here in your native place the things that we heard were done in Capernaum.'" [24]And he said, "Amen, I say to you, no prophet is accepted in his own native place. [25]Indeed, I tell you, there were many widows in Israel in the days of Elijah when the sky was closed for three and a half years and a severe famine spread over the entire land. [26]It was to none of these that Elijah was sent, but only to a widow in Zarephath in the land of Sidon. [27]Again, there were many lepers in Israel during

continue

the time of Elisha the prophet; yet not one of them was cleansed, but only Naaman the Syrian." [28]When the people in the synagogue heard this, they were all filled with fury. [29]They rose up, drove him out of the town, and led him to the brow of the hill on which their town had been built, to hurl him down headlong. [30]But he passed through the midst of them and went away.

The Cure of a Demoniac

[31]Jesus then went down to Capernaum, a town of Galilee. He taught them on the sabbath, [32]and they were astonished at his teaching because he spoke with authority. [33]In the synagogue there was a man with the spirit of an unclean demon, and he cried out in a loud voice, [34]"Ha! What have you to do with us, Jesus of Nazareth? Have you come to destroy us? I know who you are—the Holy One of God!" [35]Jesus rebuked him and said, "Be quiet! Come out of him!" Then the demon threw the man down in front of them and came out of him without doing him any harm. [36]They were all amazed and said to one another, "What is there about his word? For with authority and power he commands the unclean spirits, and they come out." [37]And news of him spread everywhere in the surrounding region.

The Cure of Simon's Mother-in-Law

[38]After he left the synagogue, he entered the house of Simon. Simon's mother-in-law was afflicted with a severe fever, and they interceded with him about her. [39]He stood over her, rebuked the fever, and it left her. She got up immediately and waited on them.

Other Healings

[40]At sunset, all who had people sick with various diseases brought them to him. He laid his hands on each of them and cured them. [41]And demons also came out from many, shouting, "You are the Son of God." But he rebuked them and did not allow them to speak because they knew that he was the Messiah.

continue

devil, Satan, and Beelzebul (see 10:18; 11:14-23) are synonymous terms for the Evil One holding creation captive. Demons, on the other hand, play a lesser role and are subject to the devil. That this exorcism as well as the following cure takes place on the sabbath is significant: the reign of God is made manifest on the literal day of the Lord, which, metaphorically speaking, is the *Day of the Lord*, the moment when the end times arrive culminating in the Lord's decisive battle with evil. When the Gospels were written, apocalyptic thought filled the thoughts of Jew and Gentile alike, and this Lukan scene reflects such a mindset. The Gospels are in a large way responsible for the fact that judgment of good and evil is an important part of the Christian theological tradition.

The cure of Simon's mother-in-law follows. The world between sickness, disease, and demonic possession was not so well defined in ancient times. None of it was good, and all of it was evil. Curing a person, therefore, would evoke the same reaction as an exorcism, a point made by the fact that Jesus "rebukes" the fever. Again, the event takes place on the sabbath, leading to the same conclusions as above. From earliest Christianity, a house located in the center of Capernaum has been held as the place of veneration commemorating this miracle, and churches have stood on the spot ever since to accommodate the thousands of pilgrims who continue to visit it.

The sabbath ends at sunset, yet people still come to Jesus for cures and exorcisms. The day of the Lord cannot be confined to the temporal cycle. The passage shows the melding of time with the eschaton. The demons always know Jesus' identity, even though the people do not, and these unclean spirits nearly always declare him the Messiah or state his divinity. Jesus prohibits them from speaking in order to demonstrate his power over them and their ruler, the devil.

Jesus leaves Capernaum at daybreak and goes to a deserted place. Tradition has often located this spot along the northeast shore of the Sea of Galilee, a place of volcanic rock and little vegetation. Luke, not known for his accuracy in Palestinian geography, ends the section by saying that Jesus goes to preach in the synagogues of Judea. This point of information is problematic. Judea is in the south. Luke's whole schema has Jesus making only one trip there, and it ends with his passion, death, and resurrection. The earliest manuscripts, Codices Sinaiticus and Vaticanus, read "Judea," but another important codex has "Galilee," the district in the north, probably written thus to resolve the narrative contradiction. Most likely Jesus made more than one journey to Judea in his lifetime. Indeed, John's Gospel indicates that Jesus went to Jerusalem at least seven times. This verse (v. 44) reflects such a tradition.

5:1-11 The miraculous draft of fish and the call of Peter

Luke is the only Synoptic writer to include the story of the miraculous catch of fish within the call of Simon, although John's Gospel shows a similar miracle in a resurrection narrative (John 21:1-11).

Lake of Gennesaret is another name for Sea of Galilee (v. 1). Fishing in the Sea of Galilee is done only at night. If the men caught nothing at that time, there was nothing to be had. That they listened to Jesus at all is indicative that they respected Jesus' opinion even when it came to their own profession. There is a tinge of doubt in Simon's reply (v. 5), and his reaction only confirms his initial skepticism (v. 8).

Jesus speaks only to Simon, and Simon is the only one to reply. Luke is preparing the reader for the leadership role that Simon (Peter) will play throughout the Lukan corpus. We get the impression that the crowd must have been so large that the only way Jesus could be seen and heard without being overwhelmed by the throng was to sit in Simon's boat just off the beach, the same boat that sails out for the catch at the Lord's command. The emphasis on Simon's boat is Luke's way of underscoring the disciple's importance on the symbolic level. Early Christian iconography often used a boat filled with people to depict the church, just as the church has long been called the "bark of Peter."

Jesus Leaves Capernaum

42 At daybreak, Jesus left and went to a deserted place. The crowds went looking for him, and when they came to him, they tried to prevent him from leaving them. 43 But he said to them, "To the other towns also I must proclaim the good news of the kingdom of God, because for this purpose I have been sent." 44 And he was preaching in the synagogues of Judea.

CHAPTER 5

The Call of Simon the Fisherman

1 While the crowd was pressing in on Jesus and listening to the word of God, he was standing by the Lake of Gennesaret. 2 He saw two boats there alongside the lake; the fishermen had disembarked and were washing their nets. 3 Getting into one of the boats, the one belonging to Simon, he asked him to put out a short distance from the shore. Then he sat down and taught the crowds from the boat. 4 After he had finished speaking, he said to Simon, "Put out into deep water and lower your nets for a catch." 5 Simon said in reply, "Master, we have worked hard all night and have caught nothing, but at your command I will lower the nets." 6 When they had done this, they caught a great number of fish and their nets were tearing. 7 They signaled to their partners in the other boat to come to help them. They came and filled both boats so that they were in danger of sinking.

continue

The miracle excites awe and wonder. Moreover, it represents the multitudinous followers this disciple will "catch" once he becomes a fisher of people in Christ's name. In verse 8 Luke uses the name "Simon Peter" for the only time and shows the disciple moved to repentance. Jesus then speaks directly to Simon in listening distance of the others. Jesus' call results in these fishermen responding immediately. They leave everything and follow, thereby becoming models of the perfect disciples.

[8]When Simon Peter saw this, he fell at the knees of Jesus and said, "Depart from me, Lord, for I am a sinful man." [9]For astonishment at the catch of fish they had made seized him and all those with him, [10]and likewise James and John, the sons of Zebedee, who were partners of Simon. Jesus said to Simon, "Do not be afraid; from now on you will be catching men." [11]When they brought their boats to the shore, they left everything and followed him.

The Cleansing of a Leper

[12]Now there was a man full of leprosy in one of the towns where he was; and when he saw Jesus, he fell prostrate, pleaded with him, and said, "Lord, if you wish, you can make me clean." [13]Jesus stretched out his hand, touched him, and said, "I do will it. Be made clean." And the leprosy left him immediately. [14]Then he ordered him not to tell anyone, but "Go, show yourself to the priest and offer for your cleansing what Moses prescribed; that will be proof for them." [15]The report about him spread all the more, and great crowds assembled to listen to him and to be cured of their ailments, [16]but he would withdraw to deserted places to pray.

continue

5:12-16 The cleansing of a leper

In the Old and New Testaments, the term "leprosy" is used to describe a variety of skin diseases, including leprosy itself. Any skin abnormalities, particularly those ulcerating or scabbing, made ritual purity impossible. Whether or not the disease was contagious, the affliction was considered a sign of sinfulness, and so people so afflicted were separated from the community to prevent physical as well as cultic contamination. After viewing the symptoms of the disease, the priests made the determination on purity or impurity (see Lev 13–14).

The man prostrates himself and acknowledges Jesus' authority both by the title "Lord"

and by the supplication "if you wish" (v. 12). His action shows his faith, which Jesus recognizes. Jesus' commanding the cleansing is an affirmation of his lordship. The injunction not to tell anyone echoes the messianic secret found in much of the Gospel of Mark. Of course, it would be impossible to keep. It shows, however, that Jesus prefers that his actions rather than his words speak of his reign. Indeed, Jesus relies on such actions as proof of his being the Messiah (Luke 7:22). As a means of evangelization, the cure has the desired affect of bringing others to Jesus. Rather than portraying Jesus as being another miracle worker among many, Luke notes that the crowds assembled first "to listen to him." Only then were they "cured of their ailments" (v. 15).

Luke, more than any other evangelist, frequently shows Jesus alone at prayer, an activity hinted at in Luke 4:42. Often Jesus retreats to a deserted place or wilderness after an intense period of preaching, healing, and exorcising, as he does here.

5:17-26 The healing of a paralytic

Although all three Synoptic Gospels have the healing of a paralytic, only Mark and Luke feature the bearers of the stretcher letting the person down through the roof. This story provides a number of details that describe the effect Jesus was having in his ministry.

The crowds he was able to draw must have been exceedingly large. The fact that Jesus teaches from a boat in Luke 5:3 gives us a hint of their size. In this passage the stretcher-bearers cannot possibly make their way through the people gathered in front of the door and must resort to unconventional methods.

Luke shows his Syrian origins here. The Markan parallel to this story says, "After they had broken through" (Mark 2:4), a statement describing better the roofs of Jewish homes in Palestine, which were flat and made of a mud-and-sod mixture resting on wooden beams or stone arches. These roofs often served as terraces on warm summer evenings. To maintain their impermeability during the rainy season, they would be rolled with a large rounded stone to compact the grasses. Burrowing a hole to let down a pallet would have been relatively easy. On the other hand, Luke states "through the tiles" (v. 19), a detail reflecting the domestic architecture stretching from the Golan Heights up into most of Syria, where a series of stone arches commonly support a roof made of shingles.

Although many see this passage as the first of several "conflict stories," there is no reason to conclude that the Pharisees and teachers of the Law are present with bad intentions, for there are no harsh words between them and Jesus until he forgives the paralytic's sins. The Pharisees are correct in their criticism—only God can forgive sins—but they do not know the full meaning of what they say. Jesus, referring to himself as the "Son of Man" for the first time in Luke (v. 24), proves his divinity with the cure, and everyone, including the Pharisees and teachers, is awestruck. Their attitude may change as Jesus progresses in his ministry, but at this point the tension is not evident. In line with the schism motif that Luke has developed (see Luke 2:34), this scene gives reason to believe that this group of Pharisees and scribes are convinced that Jesus does have such authority.

As an Aramaic phrase, the title "Son of Man" can be loosely translated by the pronoun "someone." It is used frequently in the Old Testament, especially in Ezekiel and Daniel. It gains specific import, however, in the latter book, which reads, "As the visions during the night continued, I saw coming with the clouds of heaven / One like a son of man. / When he reached the Ancient of Days / and was presented before him, / He received dominion, splendor, and kingship; / all nations, peoples, and tongues will serve him. / His dominion is an everlasting dominion / that shall not pass away, / his kingship, one that shall not be destroyed" (7:13-14). This quotation from Daniel is seminal for formation of the Christian understanding of Jesus' identity, and it is this reference, combined with the cure, which causes the crowd and the Pharisees to be awestruck.

The Healing of a Paralytic

[17]One day as Jesus was teaching, Pharisees and teachers of the law were sitting there who had come from every village of Galilee and Judea and Jerusalem, and the power of the Lord was with him for healing. [18]And some men brought on a stretcher a man who was paralyzed; they were trying to bring him in and set [him] in his presence. [19]But not finding a way to bring him in because of the crowd, they went up on the roof and lowered him on the stretcher through the tiles into the middle in front of Jesus. [20]When he saw their faith, he said, "As for you, your sins are forgiven." [21]Then the scribes and Pharisees began to ask themselves, "Who is this who speaks blasphemies? Who but God alone can forgive sins?" [22]Jesus knew their thoughts and said to them in reply, "What are you thinking in your hearts? [23]Which is easier, to say, 'Your sins are forgiven,' or to say, 'Rise and walk'? [24]But that you may know that the Son of Man has authority on earth to forgive sins"—he said to the man who was paralyzed, "I say to you, rise, pick up your stretcher, and go home." [25]He stood up immediately before them, picked up what he had been lying on, and went home, glorifying God. [26]Then astonishment seized them all and they glorified God, and, struck with awe, they said, "We have seen incredible things today."

continue

They are able to make the connection between the miracle and the person performing it.

The event itself is a good example of the incarnational character of Jesus' mission. Forgiveness of sins and spiritual well-being are not separated from physical wholeness and restoration. The Son of Man does not ignore the material world or the suffering of those living in it. By the double action of forgiving sins and curing the paralysis, Jesus shows that God's beloved creatures are redeemed in this life as well as the next.

The Call of Levi

[27]After this he went out and saw a tax collector named Levi sitting at the customs post. He said to him, "Follow me." [28]And leaving everything behind, he got up and followed him. [29]Then Levi gave a great banquet for him in his house, and a large crowd of tax collectors and others were at table with them. [30]The Pharisees and their scribes complained to his disciples, saying, "Why do you eat and drink with tax collectors and sinners?" [31]Jesus said to them in reply, "Those who are healthy do not need a physician, but the sick do. [32]I have not come to call the righteous to repentance but sinners."

continue

5:27-32 The call of Levi, the tax collector

The Jewish people detested tax collectors for good reason. On the religious level, tax collectors made themselves idolaters by cooperating with the Romans; thus they at least tacitly acclaimed Caesar's lordship. Dealing with Roman coinage, which featured an engraving of the emperor, would support such an accusation. On the nationalistic plane, by working for the Romans, Jewish tax collectors betrayed their people. They received their positions by bidding themselves out as agents to the Roman State. The Romans assessed the sum a district should provide to the emperor; the Roman officials demanded a surcharge for themselves, and the collectors were bound to bring in both while taking any extra as their remuneration. They could and would sell whole families into slavery in order to meet their demands. This position made them extortionists, both symbolically and literally.

All three Synoptic Gospels contain this story. Levi sits at the "customs post" (*telōnion* in Greek). This detail tells us that Levi taxed goods going from one political jurisdiction to another. Since nearly eighty percent of Jesus' ministry occurs along the northern shore of the Sea of Galilee, this customs post was most likely located at the mouth of the Jordan River, which formed the border between Galilee, under Herod Antipas, and Gaulanitis, under his brother Philip. The alacrity with which Levi leaves his post at the customs house indicates that his heart was predisposed to conversion before his encounter with Christ; Jesus' call is the catalyst causing the move toward repentance.

Levi's great banquet (*dochē* in Greek) with a large number of invitees underscores his wealth (v. 29). Luke's version differs from the Matthean (9:9-13) and Markan (2:13-17) accounts in several ways. Whereas the other two Synoptics specify that the Pharisees and scribes see Jesus in attendance and then speak to his disciples, Luke simply states that the Pharisees "complained" to his disciples, which leads one to believe that they were at the celebration. Were the Pharisees invited and only saw the rest of the company when they arrived? Would they have gone to a tax collector's banquet in the first place? Whatever the answer, Luke wants the reader to know that the Pharisees were in close proximity to Jesus. Unlike the preceding passage of the paralytic, where friction is not necessarily evident between Jesus and the Pharisees, here Luke describes the encounter between the two with the use of the Greek verb *gongyzō*, "to grumble against someone" or "complain," indicating that some visible tension has arisen between them (v. 30).

The parallel accounts in the other two Synoptics show "Matthew" and "Levi, son of Alphaeus" as the names of the tax collector, but Luke reads "Levi," a name suggesting that he comes from a Levitical family and therefore would have some kind of priestly function (see Deut 31:9; Josh 13:14). Certainly Luke could have shortened Mark's reading by dropping the identifier "son of Alphaeus." The name "Levi" itself, however, contains overtones of the impending messianic age.

In Malachi 3:3 we read, "and he will purify the Levites, / Refining them like gold or silver, / that they may bring offerings to the LORD in righteousness." This prophet emphasizes the impending Day of the Lord as well as the point that a messenger will come to prepare the way (Mal 3:1). Luke gives attention to John the Baptist as well as to the Day of the Lord. That Levi leaves his functions at the customs post is a sign that this remarkable day has arrived. Hence the feast, which the now repentant Levi holds, prefigures the heavenly banquet. By calling this former tax collector to a new life, the Lord Jesus has purified the sons of Levi. Note as well that with this passage Luke has blended the ministries of the Baptist and Jesus.

5:33-39 Feasting and fasting, new and old

Comparing the three Synoptic versions of this story, we see that Matthew has the disciples of John the Baptist asking Jesus why his disciples do not fast (Matt 9:14). Mark has "people" inquiring, but with a reference to both John's disciples and the Pharisees (Mark 2:18). Luke is obviously editing material that has come through Mark. The antecedent of the pronoun "they" (Luke 5:33) is difficult to identify. Since further on in the verse there is mention of the Pharisees in the third person, "the disciples of the Pharisees do the same," it would seem that the scribes are asking the question. As a professional class of writers who knew the written law, they would not necessarily be as prone to follow the oral traditions promulgated by the Pharisees, even though they may have very well been aware of them.

In addition, the thematic content supports the scribes as the ones interrogating Jesus. This question about eating habits follows within the context of Levi's great banquet (Luke 5:27-32). A similar controversy over feasting and fasting arises further on in Jesus' ministry (Luke 7:31-35). It seems obvious that Jesus has developed a reputation for being one who enjoys good food and wine, and according to the Gospel account, this accusation is not without basis. Not only does he use banquet imagery in much of his preaching, but he is frequently seen at dinner feasts with Pharisees, tax collectors, and sinners. Indeed, Jesus refers to himself as a bridegroom in this passage, thus making his ministry on earth a wedding banquet filled

The Question about Fasting

³³And they said to him, "The disciples of John fast often and offer prayers, and the disciples of the Pharisees do the same; but yours eat and drink." ³⁴Jesus answered them, "Can you make the wedding guests fast while the bridegroom is with them? ³⁵But the days will come, and when the bridegroom is taken away from them, then they will fast in those days." ³⁶And he also told them a parable. "No one tears a piece from a new cloak to patch an old one. Otherwise, he will tear the new and the piece from it will not match the old cloak. ³⁷Likewise, no one pours new wine into old wineskins. Otherwise, the new wine will burst the skins, and it will be spilled, and the skins will be ruined. ³⁸Rather, new wine must be poured into fresh wineskins. ³⁹[And] no one who has been drinking old wine desires new, for he says, 'The old is good.'"

with the joy and the promise of new life. It is the Day of the Lord.

This passage reflects the tensions existing between the Christian movement and Pharisaic Judaism. Although Luke goes to great lengths to demonstrate Christianity's roots in Jewish tradition, particularly in the prophets (see Luke 1–2), the religious practices of the early Pharisees and Christians were incompatible. This irreconcilability stands as the background to the passage.

The parable about new and old patches, cloaks, and wineskins has a twist. The lesson about cloth and wineskins is easy to follow, and the conclusions are based on common sense. One uses old cloth to patch new, not vice versa; the fermentation of new wine needs the elasticity of new skins, not the brittleness of old ones. The summarizing statement, a verse that only Luke shows, however, is ironic: "[And] no one who has been drinking old wine desires new, for he says, 'The old is good'"

(v. 39). After a discourse on the desirability of leaving the old for the new, Jesus concludes by admitting that we often prefer the comfort of the old to the challenges of the new, particularly when we see nothing wrong or bad with the old. On the other hand, the examination of the metaphor shows that, in this case, there is something wrong and bad about the old. Threadbare clothing is of little use to anyone, and wineskins can be used only once. We must not let comfort and security blind us to the blessings of the kingdom.

Jesus' point is that the life of a disciple is not a dour regimen of religious protocol, but a life of joy. We should not let self-complacency blind us to the banquet the Bridegroom has ushered in, a banquet that begins now even as we wait to see its fullness in the yet-to-come.

EXPLORING LESSON THREE

1. Why do you think the crowds flocked to John the Baptist (3:1-15)? Do you think you might have been among them at the time?

_____

_____

_____

_____

_____

2. Who does the heavenly voice address at Jesus' baptism in Matthew 3:17? In Luke 3:22? How do these differences affect the impact of the message?

_____

_____

_____

_____

_____

_____

3. What does Luke's genealogy of Jesus (3:23-38) emphasize that is not as apparent in Matthew's genealogy (1:1-17)?

_____

_____

_____

_____

4. a) What do the three temptations of Jesus represent in Luke (4:1-13)?

_____

_____

b) Where do you see Jesus' followers experiencing these same temptations today?

_____

_____

_____

5. How does the response to Jesus' proclamation of the prophet Isaiah in his hometown synagogue (4:16-30) demonstrate the theme of schism in Luke?

_____

_____

_____

_____

_____

_____

6. Why would Jesus refuse to let the demons proclaim him as the Messiah (4:40-41)?

_____

_____

_____

_____

_____

7. What does Jesus tell the crowds in Capernaum about the purpose of his ministry (4:42-44)? What does that mean to you?

_____

_____

_____

_____

_____

8. Other than Jesus, who is the most prominent figure in Luke 5:1-11? What reasons might there be for his prominence there and elsewhere in Luke?

_____

_____

_____

_____

_____

9. The friends of the paralytic went to great lengths to get their friend to Jesus (5:17-21). Recall a time when a friend (or stranger who acted as a true friend) went to great lengths to help you.

_____

_____

_____

_____

_____

_____

10. What is significant about Jesus referring to himself as the bridegroom (5:33-35)? (See Isa 54:4-8; 62:5.)

_____

_____

_____

_____

_____

_____

See next page for closing prayer.

CLOSING PRAYER

Prayer

The report about him spread all the more, and great crowds assembled to listen to him and to be cured of their ailments, but he would withdraw to deserted places to pray.

(Luke 5:15-16)

Healing Jesus, teach us to balance the good we do with the time we need simply to be with you. Call us to come away for prayer and then send us as agents of your healing. We pray this week for those who are ill, especially . . .

LESSON FOUR

Luke 6–7

Begin your personal study and group discussion with a simple and sincere prayer such as:

Prayer

O God of Joy, send your Spirit with a freshness that will help me hear familiar words with open ears and heart. Guide me as I pray and study the Gospel of Luke.

Read the Bible text of Luke 6–7, found in the outside columns of pages 52–60, highlighting what stands out to you.

Read the accompanying commentary to add to your understanding.

Respond to the questions on pages 62–64, Exploring Lesson Four.

The closing prayer on page 64 is for your personal use and may be used at the end of group discussion.

CHAPTER 6

Debates about the Sabbath

[1]While he was going through a field of grain on a sabbath, his disciples were picking the heads of grain, rubbing them in their hands, and eating them. [2]Some Pharisees said, "Why are you doing what is unlawful on the sabbath?" [3]Jesus said to them in reply, "Have you not read what David did when he and those [who were] with him were hungry? [4][How] he went into the house of God, took the bread of offering, which only the priests could lawfully eat, ate of it, and shared it with his companions." [5]Then he said to them, "The Son of Man is lord of the sabbath."

[6]On another sabbath he went into the synagogue and taught, and there was a man there whose right hand was withered. [7]The scribes and the Pharisees watched him closely to see if he would cure on the sabbath so that they might discover a reason to accuse him. [8]But he realized their intentions and said to the man with the withered hand, "Come up and stand before us." And he rose and stood there. [9]Then Jesus said to them, "I ask you, is it lawful to do good on the

continue

6:1-11 Debates about the sabbath

The Mosaic prohibition against work on the sabbath recurs in many places throughout the Pentateuch. The legislation first surfaces in Exodus 16:23-29, where Moses directs the Israelites on how to collect the manna the Lord has given them. They are to gather enough for the day at hand and leave none for the next day. This instruction is in force until the sixth day, when they are to gather twice as much for the following sabbath. Interestingly, when some disobey Moses by keeping some manna longer than they are supposed to, the cache becomes rotten and wormy. When the leftovers are saved for the sabbath, however, the manna remains edible. This Exodus account gives rise to further legislation and consequent debates on what constitutes work on the sabbath.

The controversy revolves around sabbath regulation. If the disciples performed a similar action on any other day of the week, they would have been within their rights (Deut 23:25). Here, however, not only are the disciples in Luke 6:1-5 violating prohibitions against harvesting fields and threshing grain, but by carrying goods, they are also guilty of breaking a sabbath law (see Num 15:32). Jesus' reply to the Pharisees is nearly the same in the other two Synoptic parallels (see Matt 12:1-8; Mark 2:23-28).

The incident to which Luke refers is found in 1 Samuel 21:1-7. Jesus' point is that Pharisees overlook David's infractions, who, with his men, is guilty of breaking more laws than the disciples are. Yet the Pharisees become indignant at Jesus for a less serious offense, and he is the Lord of the sabbath. This moment is one of messianic revelation, but the Pharisees' legalism blinds them to it. The passage ends with "The Son of Man is lord of the sabbath" (v. 5), a verse that introduces another story on violating the sabbath.

The issue at hand is not that Jesus cures but that he cures on the sabbath, something that is considered work. As with the exorcism of the demoniac (Luke 4:31-37), the sabbath or Lord's Day here is also considered the eschatological Day of the Lord, when suffering will cease and wholeness will be restored. Jesus tries to make that point when he addresses the assembly (v. 9), and he proves his lordship in restoring the man's withered hand (v. 10). Seeing that Jesus' argument and actions are unassailable, the scribes and Pharisees become incensed.

It is important to note that Jesus' conflicts with the Pharisees reflect more the tension within the early Christian community concerning Jews and Jewish practice than they do between Jesus and the Jews. Both Jews and Gentiles saw themselves as followers of Christ, and passages such as these show the points of contention both inside and outside the Christian community. Thus, when Jesus castigates the Pharisees in this passage, we see and hear the early debates within the Jewish-Christian community.

6:12-16 The mission of the Twelve

There is a noticeable shift of direction in this scene. Away from the synagogues, towns, and people, Jesus goes "to the mountain to pray" (v. 12) in an all-night vigil. The exact mountain is unknown, though the use of the definite article indicates that Lukan tradition must have had some specific mountain in mind. Galilee has many high places that could qualify as quiet retreats for prayer, but two are the most likely promontories: Mount Hermon, rising from the northeast corner of the Sea of Galilee, and Mount Tabor, south of the sea, visible from Nazareth and on the Jezreel Plain. They both have been traditional places of prayer from earliest antiquity (see Ps 89:13), although Tabor is the more accessible of the two.

Jesus selects from all his disciples twelve men who will have a share in his ministry. The names of the Twelve do not match the lists of the other Gospels, nor do they correspond with what Luke writes in his second volume (see Acts 1:13). In fact, none of the lists in the Synoptics are in exact agreement with each other. How do we account for the fact that the apostles (and only Luke and Matthew call these men apostles) differ, especially when the early church placed so much emphasis on apostolic foundation in determining whether

sabbath rather than to do evil, to save life rather than to destroy it?" [10]Looking around at them all, he then said to him, "Stretch out your hand." He did so and his hand was restored. [11]But they became enraged and discussed together what they might do to Jesus.

The Mission of the Twelve

[12]In those days he departed to the mountain to pray, and he spent the night in prayer to God. [13]When day came, he called his disciples to himself, and from them he chose Twelve, whom he also named apostles: [14]Simon, whom he named Peter, and his brother Andrew, James, John, Philip, Bartholomew, [15]Matthew, Thomas, James the son of Alphaeus, Simon who was called a Zealot, [16]and Judas the son of James, and Judas Iscariot, who became a traitor.

Ministering to a Great Multitude

[17]And he came down with them and stood on a stretch of level ground. A great crowd of his disciples and a large number of the people from all Judea and Jerusalem and the coastal region of

continue

a community was orthodox or that its writings should be included in the canon? One suggestion for the variety of names is that each Gospel writer is recalling the representative figures peculiar to the community for which he is writing. These figures may have known or worked with one or more of what came to be called "the Twelve." All four Gospels agree that Judas Iscariot betrays Jesus, however.

After the night in prayer, Jesus returns to his ministry, except now the people come to him.

6:17-19 Ministering to a great multitude

The crowd's various lands of origin give the reader insight into Luke's geographical understanding as well as his theological agenda. The commission described in Acts 1:8

Tyre and Sidon [18]came to hear him and to be healed of their diseases; and even those who were tormented by unclean spirits were cured. [19]Everyone in the crowd sought to touch him because power came forth from him and healed them all.

Sermon on the Plain

[20]And raising his eyes toward his disciples he said:

"Blessed are you who are poor,
for the kingdom of God is yours.
[21]Blessed are you who are now hungry,
for you will be satisfied.
Blessed are you who are now weeping,
for you will laugh.
[22]Blessed are you when people hate you,
and when they exclude and insult you,
and denounce your name as evil
on account of the Son of Man.

[23]Rejoice and leap for joy on that day! Behold, your reward will be great in heaven. For their ancestors treated the prophets in the same way.

[24]But woe to you who are rich,
for you have received your consolation.
[25]But woe to you who are filled now,
for you will be hungry.
Woe to you who laugh now,
for you will grieve and weep.
[26]Woe to you when all speak well of you,
for their ancestors treated the false
prophets in this way.

Love of Enemies

[27]"But to you who hear I say, love your enemies, do good to those who hate you, [28]bless those who curse you, pray for those who mistreat you. [29]To the person who strikes you on one cheek, offer the other one as well, and from the person who takes your cloak, do not withhold even your tunic. [30]Give to everyone who asks of you, and from the one who takes what is yours do not demand it

continue

reads: "you will be my witnesses in Jerusalem, throughout Judea and Samaria, and to the ends of the earth." In the Acts of the Apostles, the apostolic mission follows that trajectory. Here in this passage, however, "Samaria" and the "ends of the earth" are not included. The explanation can be found in Luke 9:52-53, where Jesus and his disciples are not welcomed in the Samaritan village. Samaria's time will come, and so will the proclamation to the ends of the earth. For now, Tyre and Sidon, as seaports and in pagan territory, represent for Luke the future direction of the Christian movement. In this passage Luke paints a picture of a mission at the threshold.

6:20-49 Sermon on the Plain

The Sermon on the Plain evidences four sections: the Beatitudes, the exhortations, the analogy of trees and fruit, and the parable of the two houses.

Beatitudes. Jesus descends the mountain before preaching. The Moses typology, so much a part of Matthew's Gospel, does not exist in Luke. He raises his eyes towards his disciples, and addresses the people (v. 20), a simple gesture that calls forth discipleship on the part of the crowd. Because Luke has his Gentile audience in mind, he does not include the *lex talionis* found in Matthew 5:38. Certainly not as quoted or well known as Matthew's Beatitudes, the Lukan redaction is also shorter. Most critics believe that both Matthew and Luke use Q as the source material for their respective versions.

The great reversal theme, first outlined in the *Magnificat* (Luke 1:46-55), recurs here: the poor will inherit the kingdom, the hungry will be satisfied, those weeping will laugh. Luke addresses the people in the second person, whereas Matthew uses the third person. For this reason, some maintain that Luke foresees an immediate resolution to the suffering of the outcast while holding that Matthew pushes justice into the eschaton. The interpretation of the Lukan Beatitudes is not that simple, however. Because the Lukan eschatological vision surfaces through the juxtaposition of the Woes in verses 24-26, there is no reason to assume that Luke sees the resolution of the tension between the blessed and the woebegone occurring only within this lifetime. Likewise, Matthew's Beatitudes challenge people to address social injustices in this world.

Luke, like Matthew, places suffering and reward within the context of the Old Testament, in which true prophets faced torture and death, while the false ones found worldly grace and favor. As the Gospel narrative continues, the reader sees Jesus encountering a similar fate. The heart of the message is that we do God's will on earth to relieve suffering and oppression, realizing all along that ultimate mercy and justice will come only with the eschaton.

back. ³¹Do to others as you would have them do to you. ³²For if you love those who love you, what credit is that to you? Even sinners love those who love them. ³³And if you do good to those who do good to you, what credit is that to you? Even sinners do the same. ³⁴If you lend money to those from whom you expect repayment, what credit [is] that to you? Even sinners lend to sinners, and get back the same amount. ³⁵But rather, love your enemies and do good to them, and lend expecting nothing back; then your reward will be great and you will be children of the Most High, for he

continue

The **beatitudes** in Luke differ from those in Matthew. Matthew has eight beatitudes poetically structured in the third person and one in the second person. In Luke, there are only four beatitudes accompanied by four woes, all in the second person. Both sets are well structured and written in parallel fashion but with different emphases. Many scholars believe Luke's version to be more original, but each has been shaped by the theological outlook of the respective evangelist. Matthew's are more spiritualized, while Luke's are concrete and emphasize the present time.

Matthew 5:3-12	Luke 6:20-26
Blessed are the poor in spirit . . .	Blessed are you . . . poor . . .
Blessed are they who mourn . . .	Blessed are you . . . now hungry . . .
Blessed are the meek . . .	Blessed are you . . . now weeping . . .
Blessed are they who hunger and thirst for righteousness . . .	Blessed are you . . . hate you and insult you . . .
Blessed are the merciful . . .	Woe to you . . . rich . . .
Blessed are the clean of heart . . .	Woe to you . . . filled now . . .
Blessed are the peacemakers . . .	Woe to you . . . laugh now . . .
Blessed are they who are persecuted for the sake of righteousness	Woe to you . . . when all speak well of you . . . for their ancestors treated the false prophets . . .
Blessed are you when they insult you and persecute you and utter every kind of evil against you [falsely] because of me	

himself is kind to the ungrateful and the wicked. [36]Be merciful, just as [also] your Father is merciful.

Judging Others

[37]"Stop judging and you will not be judged. Stop condemning and you will not be condemned. Forgive and you will be forgiven. [38]Give and gifts will be given to you; a good measure, packed together, shaken down, and overflowing, will be poured into your lap. For the measure with which you measure will in return be measured out to you." [39]And he told them a parable, "Can a blind person guide a blind person? Will not both fall into a pit? [40]No disciple is superior to the teacher; but when fully trained, every disciple will be like his teacher. [41]Why do you notice the splinter in your brother's eye, but do not perceive the wooden beam in your own? [42]How can you say to your brother, 'Brother, let me remove that splinter in your eye,' when you do not even notice the wooden beam in your own eye? You hypocrite! Remove the wooden beam from your eye first; then you will see clearly to remove the splinter in your brother's eye.

A Tree Known by Its Fruit

[43]"A good tree does not bear rotten fruit, nor does a rotten tree bear good fruit. [44]For every tree is known by its own fruit. For people do not pick figs from thornbushes, nor do they gather grapes from brambles. [45]A good person out of the store of goodness in his heart produces good, but an evil person out of a store of evil produces evil; for from the fullness of the heart the mouth speaks.

The Two Foundations

[46]"Why do you call me, 'Lord, Lord,' but not do what I command? [47]I will show you what someone is like who comes to me, listens to my words, and acts on them. [48]That one is like a person building a house, who dug deeply and laid the foundation on rock; when the flood came, the

continue

Exhortations. Luke goes to great lengths in explaining love of enemies (vv. 27-38). Human love should match divine love, a love that is "kind to the ungrateful and the wicked" (v. 35). This call to be "merciful, just as [also] your Father is merciful" (v. 36) is a particular Lukan characteristic. Because Luke defines so well the boundless quality of divine mercy, Dante refers to the evangelist as the *Scritsa mansuetudinis Christi*, the "narrator of the sweet gentleness of Christ."

The lesson on judging others is connected to love of enemies. The context surrounding the admonition not to judge others does not refer to assessing the rightness or wrongness of an action or of its moral content; obviously, the whole of the Beatitudes contains elements of judgment. Rather, Luke is addressing those who would play the part of God by judging the salvation or damnation of others, something only God can do. For those who would assume to take on that role, Luke offers a stern warning: they may end up condemning themselves. Similarly, those who extend the benefit of the doubt will have manifold blessings extended to them (v. 38).

Analogy. This comparison of a tree and its fruit is Q material. Matthew contains a nearly identical passage (Matt 7:16-20), but it is not as concise as the one we read here. The image of good and bad fruit and its association with prophecy echo several Old Testament prophetic utterances. Jeremiah performs an action of the good and bad figs (Jer 24:1-10), and a central metaphor for Isaiah (5:1-7) is the vine and grapes. Ezekiel has something similar (Ezek 19:10-14). Thus this short section functions as a reprise for Luke's reference to true and false prophets (vv. 23 and 26).

Parable. The comparison of the two houses (vv. 46-49; Matt 7:21-27) yields readings that reflect the geography of the two different communities. In Syria one would have to dig to reach the bedrock upon which to build; in Palestine and Israel, the bedrock is exposed. Syria has permanent rivers and streams running through it. Indeed, Antioch is situated on the Orontes, just one of several rivers in Syria.

On the other hand, the country about which Matthew writes has only the Jordan, and no real city stands on its banks. The house for Matthew, therefore, is destroyed by wind and rain. The point in both readings, however, is the same: for one to follow Jesus, there must be care, determination, and full intention. The halfhearted who would try to be a disciple will simply wash away.

7:1-10 Healing the centurion's slave at Capernaum

Although Luke shares this story with Matthew, Luke's difference is most notable in that the evangelist includes the Jewish emissaries who are very supportive of the centurion. Several features draw our attention.

The centurion, as the name implies, was in charge of one hundred men. At this time in history, Romans ruled the country through their clients, with Galilee and Perea under the jurisdiction of Herod Antipas. Hence the centurion need not have been a Roman, even though he was a Gentile. That he was a Gentile, however, would have entailed difficulties enough, for a Jew could not enter a Gentile home without becoming ritually impure.

There are two words in Greek used for the term "slave." One is *doulos*, and the other is *pais*. In verses 2, 3, 8, and 10, Luke uses *doulos*, and in verse 7 we read *pais*. Of the two words, the latter, which literally means "boy" or "youth," describes a more personal, endearing relationship. On the other hand, *doulos* expresses the servility associated with such a state. The translation here, with its use of "slave" and "servant" in the respective verses, shows the nuance between the two words. Luke contrasts the two terms in the narrative. When using indirect address, as in verses 2, 3, and 10, or when the centurion speaks in the abstract, as in verse 8, the text shows *doulos*. When Luke quotes the centurion, however, he employs the term *pais*. From this juxtaposition we can see that Luke is emphasizing the kinship the centurion feels for his servant.

The interplay between the Jewish elders and the centurion is notable. Although the

river burst against that house but could not shake it because it had been well built. [49]But the one who listens and does not act is like a person who built a house on the ground without a foundation. When the river burst against it, it collapsed at once and was completely destroyed."

CHAPTER 7

The Healing of a Centurion's Slave

[1]When he had finished all his words to the people, he entered Capernaum. [2]A centurion there had a slave who was ill and about to die, and he was valuable to him. [3]When he heard about Jesus, he sent elders of the Jews to him, asking him to come and save the life of his slave. [4]They approached Jesus and strongly urged him to come, saying, "He deserves to have you do this for him, [5]for he loves our nation and he built the synagogue for us." [6]And Jesus went with them, but when he was only a short distance from the house, the centurion sent friends to tell him, "Lord, do not trouble yourself, for I am not worthy to have you enter under my roof. [7]Therefore, I did not consider myself worthy to come to you; but say the word and let my servant be healed. [8]For I too am a person subject to authority, with soldiers subject to me. And I say to one, 'Go,' and he goes; and to another, 'Come here,' and he comes; and to my slave, 'Do this,' and he does it." [9]When Jesus heard this he was amazed at him and, turning, said to the crowd following him, "I tell you, not even in Israel have I found such faith." [10]When the messengers returned to the house, they found the slave in good health.

continue

centurion is in service to the nominally Jewish tetrarch, Herod Antipas, he is still a Gentile. Herod Antipas, as a Roman client, has to pay tribute to the Romans, and he passes on this expense by levying heavy taxes upon the population. Nonetheless, the picture we have here shows some semblance of mutual respect between the two parties. The Jewish elders say

Raising of the Widow's Son

[11]Soon afterward he journeyed to a city called Nain, and his disciples and a large crowd accompanied him. [12]As he drew near to the gate of the city, a man who had died was being carried out, the only son of his mother, and she was a widow. A large crowd from the city was with her. [13]When the Lord saw her, he was moved with pity for her and said to her, "Do not weep." [14]He stepped forward and touched the coffin; at this the bearers halted, and he said, "Young man, I tell you, arise!" [15]The dead man sat up and began to speak, and Jesus gave him to his mother. [16]Fear seized them all, and they glorified God, exclaiming, "A great prophet has arisen in our midst," and "God has visited his people." [17]This report about him spread through the whole of Judea and in all the surrounding region.

The Messengers from John the Baptist

[18]The disciples of John told him about all these things. John summoned two of his disciples [19]and sent them to the Lord to ask, "Are you the one who is to come, or should we look for another?" [20]When the men came to him, they said, "John the Baptist has sent us to you to ask, 'Are you the one who is to come, or should we look for another?'" [21]At that time he cured many of their diseases, sufferings, and evil spirits; he also granted sight to many who were blind. [22]And he said to them in reply, "Go and tell John what you have seen and heard: the blind regain their sight, the lame walk, lepers are cleansed, the deaf hear, the dead are raised, the poor have the good news proclaimed to them. [23]And blessed is the one who takes no offense at me."

Jesus' Testimony to John

[24]When the messengers of John had left, Jesus began to speak to the crowds about John. "What did you go out to the desert to see—a reed swayed by the wind? [25]Then what did you go out to see? Someone dressed in fine garments? Those who

continue

that the centurion "loves our nation and he built the synagogue for us" (v. 5). Furthermore, the centurion exhibits all the signs of faith in the Lord God that the religious Jew shows. It seems that Luke has described a "God-fearer," a Gentile who found the monotheistic God of the Jews and their moral code appealing, but who was unable or unwilling to separate himself from his own family and ethnic group by dietary laws or circumcision (see Acts 10:22). Thus the Jewish elders in verse 4 can speak highly of the centurion. In addition, knowing that a religious Jew could not enter a Gentile house, the centurion obviates a potentially embarrassing situation by sending a second band of emissaries, this time "friends," with the advice that Jesus perform his deed from afar. Luke probably included this passage to support the place of Gentiles within the Jewish-Christian movement. As Jesus comes to the Gentile centurion, so, too, does he come to Gentiles in the Mediterranean world.

Finally, we see a positive exchange between the Jewish elders and Jesus. Although Luke often describes a great deal of tension between Pharisaical parties and Jesus, the relationship between Jesus and the Jews is not always hostile, as we see here. The elders may not be Pharisees specifically but may have some position of authority in the community, indicating some degree of formal adherence to the Mosaic Law.

The ruins of the second-century synagogue in Capernaum rest on a foundation of an earlier one, which according to one tradition is the synagogue in question here.

7:11-17 The son of the widow of Nain

This story is found only in Luke, and it is the first occurrence of restoring the dead to life found in this Gospel.

Tradition locates Nain on the southwest side of the Carmel mountain range in Galilee. That the prophet Elisha performed a similar miracle in Shunem, on the northeast side of the same mountain range, no doubt influences the response of the crowd here (see 2 Kgs 4:8-37); they exclaim, "A great prophet has arisen in our midst" (v. 16). Some commentators also see an allusion to Elijah's raising the son of the widow of Zarephath, near Sidon in present-day Lebanon (1 Kgs 17:8-24).

In both these accounts the respective prophet resuscitates the dead by lying on top of them several times, and this point highlights the difference they have with the story involving Jesus at Nain. Here Jesus simply commands the young man to rise. The action reflects Jesus' authority, and the crowd recognizes this fact.

7:18-23 The messengers from John the Baptist

This passage is the first formal encounter between John the Baptist and Jesus. Though John baptizes Jesus in 3:21-22, he does so unknowingly. The infancy narratives show the accounts dealing with the Baptist preceding those of Jesus; for example, the annunciation to Zechariah and John's birth come before the annunciation to Mary and Jesus' birth in Bethlehem. This pattern emphasizes that John the Baptist is not the Messiah, but the precursor to the Messiah. Such an understanding is underscored at the baptism and is further clarified here. John the Baptist has seen himself as the forerunner (see 3:16-17). In sending disciples to ask such a question of Jesus now, he seeks confirmation that Jesus is the Messiah for whom he has prepared the way.

The Baptist's disciples in this narrative also play a role for the early church. At this time (A.D. 80–90) and even later, there was tension between the followers of John and those of Jesus. Luke's construction of having John's disciples asking Jesus if they "should . . . look for another" (vv. 19-20) serves as the Christian community's invitation to the Baptist's disciples to join the ranks of Jesus' followers.

Jesus' answer to the Baptist's messengers is based on his ministry thus far, including the raising of the dead, as seen at Nain, which Luke places immediately before this passage. Jesus' response draws on Old Testament prophecy, especially the sayings of the prophet Isaiah (29:18-19; 35:5-6; 61:1), whose preaching is echoed in the synagogue at Nazareth (see

dress luxuriously and live sumptuously are found in royal palaces. [26]Then what did you go out to see? A prophet? Yes, I tell you, and more than a prophet. [27]This is the one about whom scripture says:

'Behold, I am sending my messenger ahead of you,
   he will prepare your way before you.'

[28]I tell you, among those born of women, no one is greater than John; yet the least in the kingdom of God is greater than he." [29](All the people who listened, including the tax collectors, and who were baptized with the baptism of John, acknowledged the righteousness of God; [30]but the Pharisees and scholars of the law, who were not baptized by him, rejected the plan of God for themselves.)

[31]"Then to what shall I compare the people of this generation? What are they like? [32]They are like children who sit in the marketplace and call to one another,

'We played the flute for you, but you did not dance.
   We sang a dirge, but you did not weep.'

continue

Luke 4:18-21). In framing his words by citations from Isaiah, we see how Judaism forms the crucial context for understanding the Gospels and the New Testament.

7:24-35 Jesus and John

Jesus' testimony about John lessens the tensions between their respective disciples as it extends a welcoming embrace to the Baptist's followers. Jesus, the true Messiah, has tremendous regard and respect for John the Baptist: "A prophet? Yes, I tell you, and more than a prophet" (7:26).

The schism motif resurfaces at verses 29-30. Some who had chosen John's baptism see the plan of God fulfilled in Jesus, and others who had rejected John's baptism also reject Jesus

³³For John the Baptist came neither eating food nor drinking wine, and you said, 'He is possessed by a demon.' ³⁴The Son of Man came eating and drinking and you said, 'Look, he is a glutton and a drunkard, a friend of tax collectors and sinners.' ³⁵But wisdom is vindicated by all her children."

The Pardon of the Sinful Woman

³⁶A Pharisee invited him to dine with him, and he entered the Pharisee's house and reclined at table. ³⁷Now there was a sinful woman in the city who learned that he was at table in the house of the Pharisee. Bringing an alabaster flask of ointment, ³⁸she stood behind him at his feet weeping and began to bathe his feet with her tears. Then she wiped them with her hair, kissed them, and anointed them with the ointment. ³⁹When the Pharisee who had invited him saw this he said to himself, "If this man were a prophet, he would know who and what sort of woman this is who is touching him, that she is a sinner." ⁴⁰Jesus said to him in reply, "Simon, I have something to say to you." "Tell me, teacher," he said. ⁴¹"Two people were in debt to a certain creditor; one owed five hundred days' wages and the other owed fifty. ⁴²Since they were unable to repay the debt, he forgave it for both. Which of them will love him more?" ⁴³Simon said in reply, "The one, I suppose, whose larger debt was forgiven." He said to him, "You have judged rightly." ⁴⁴Then he turned to the woman and said to Simon, "Do you see this woman? When I entered your house, you did not give me water for my feet, but she has bathed them with her tears and wiped them with her hair. ⁴⁵You did not give me a kiss, but she has not ceased kissing my feet since the time I entered. ⁴⁶You did not anoint my head with oil, but she anointed my feet with ointment. ⁴⁷So I tell you, her many sins have been forgiven; hence, she has shown great love. But the one to whom little is forgiven, loves little." ⁴⁸He said to her, "Your sins are forgiven." ⁴⁹The others at table said to themselves, "Who is this who even forgives sins?" ⁵⁰But he said to the woman, "Your faith has saved you; go in peace."

and his message. In this latter group, Jesus mentions specifically Pharisees and scholars of the Law. The analogy of the children in the marketplace (vv. 31-32) is apt for them. No matter what the message or the deed, many people will find fault with God's design, because accepting the will of God necessitates a change in one's behavior. It would be wrong to assume that no Pharisees or scribes were disciples either of John or of Jesus; the reign of God split that group as well (see 7:1-10, 36-50; 13:31-33; 14:1-6). The hardness of heart they exhibit here crosses all class divisions.

Lest we tend to overlook the joy Jesus had in his earthly life, it would be good to note that he seems to have had the reputation of relishing good food and drink, as verses 33-34 suggest (see also 5:30; 7:36-50; 10:38-42). In addition, many of his parables and allusions are based on feasting metaphors (see 14:7-14, 15-24). As seen throughout Luke's Gospel, attention to conversion, concern for the poor, and enjoyment of all God's gifts go hand in hand. A dour disciple does not further the reign of God.

7:36-50 The woman of loving gratitude

It is often assumed that the woman is guilty of some kind of sexual sin, yet there is nothing in the text to suggest such a conclusion. The material concerning John the Baptist ("the poor have the good news proclaimed to them"— 7:22) forms a good context for this passage. In the tradition this story becomes entangled with Matthew 26:6-13; Mark 14:3-9; John 12:1-8, all recording the anointing at Bethany on the journey to Jerusalem. In Luke, Jesus does not turn toward Jerusalem until 9:51, so this occasion, in the Lukan literary outline at least, is set in Galilee.

Simon the Pharisee's lack of attention to the details of hospitality notwithstanding, such an incident would be shocking in any case. Guests would have been reclining around the outside rim of a *triclinium*, a horseshoe-shaped table. While the left side of their torsos rested on elevated cushions to allow them to take food and drink with their right hand, their feet would be exposed to the wall's perimeter. Before the second century, the Roman custom was to have the *triclinium* open or near the *atrium*. Such an arrangement would explain how the woman gained access to the house. Nonetheless, she would have had to crawl around the outside rim of the table until she found the right set of feet before she could start the anointing. Even with the broadest, most accepting, and opened mind and heart, and even within the public culture of the Mideast, her actions would have been seen as suspicious or at least bizarre. Simon's consternation is understandable, if not permissible.

The text does not mention what kind of ointment the woman uses, but if it is contained in an alabaster jar, it would have been very expensive. The juxtaposition of using this ointment on the feet when the guest should have been anointed on the head accentuates the great release of guilt and shame this woman feels from having encountered Jesus somewhere along the way.

Jesus does not defend the woman by saying that she is sinless; rather, he acknowledges her sins and forgives them. The parable forms the interpretation of the event. Everyone is a sinner and everyone needs forgiveness. Only when we realize that we need the grace of Christ, do we see what a great gift the forgiveness is. This woman becomes the model of the proper response of limitless gratitude all people should show in light of the salvation Christ offers.

Simon's inner thoughts (v. 39) have an ironic twist. Jesus *is* a prophet, and he *does* know what kind of woman this is. That is why he responds in such a manner.

EXPLORING LESSON FOUR

1. Why was the behavior of Jesus and his disciples during the Sabbath such a contentious matter for the scribes and the Pharisees (6:1-11)? (See Exod 16:23-29; 20:8-11.)

_____

_____

_____

_____

_____

2. How is the theme of "the great reversal" made apparent in Luke's Sermon on the Plain (6:20-26)?

_____

_____

_____

_____

_____

3. Why do some think Luke's beatitudes and woes should be interpreted as belonging to this life and not just to the life hereafter (6:20-26)? Why might they be thought of as belonging to the end of time (the eschaton)?

_____

_____

_____

_____

_____

4. What cultural messages (or personal experiences) make love of enemy (6:27-36) so challenging? How could you become more open to such love?

_____

_____

_____

_____

_____

5. What life experiences have taught you the wisdom found in the teaching of Jesus in Luke 6:41-42?

_____

_____

_____

_____

_____

6. What reasons could the centurion have had to claim unworthiness for either coming to Jesus himself or having Jesus enter his home (7:1-10)? When have you experienced God working in your life even when you have felt unworthy?

_____

_____

_____

_____

_____

7. The crowds recalled the prophetic careers of Elijah and Elisha when Jesus raised the widow of Nain's son from the dead (7:11-16; see 1 Kgs 17:8-24; 2 Kgs 4:8-37). Why?

_____

_____

_____

_____

_____

8. Your commentary indicates that Judaism is "the crucial context for understanding the gospels." How does Jesus' response to the question of John's disciples (7:18-23) illustrate that insight?

_____

_____

_____

_____

_____

9. What do you make of Jesus' self-disclosure that he took pleasure in good food, drink, and the company of others (7:31-35)?

_____

_____

_____

_____

_____

10. How do the circumstances surrounding the woman's expression of love for Jesus demonstrate both humility and courage (7:36-50)?

_____

_____

_____

_____

_____

CLOSING PRAYER

Prayer

"Go and tell John what you have seen and heard: the blind regain their sight, the lame walk, lepers are cleansed, the deaf hear, the dead are raised, the poor have the good news proclaimed to them."   (Luke 7:22)

Jesus, made manifest in your church, prod us to give others something to talk about—healings, care, compassion. Help us to live the Good News and not merely preach it. We pray for these works of the faithful done in your name, that we call by name now . . .

LESSON FIVE

Luke 8:1–9:50

Begin your personal study and group discussion with a simple and sincere prayer such as:

Prayer

O God of Joy, send your Spirit with a freshness that will help me hear familiar words with open ears and heart. Guide me as I pray and study the Gospel of Luke.

Read the Bible text of Luke 8:1–9:50, found in the outside columns of pages 66–76, highlighting what stands out to you.

Read the accompanying commentary to add to your understanding.

Respond to the questions on pages 77–79, Exploring Lesson Five.

The closing prayer on page 80 is for your personal use and may be used at the end of group discussion.

CHAPTER 8

Galilean Women Follow Jesus

[1]Afterward he journeyed from one town and village to another, preaching and proclaiming the good news of the kingdom of God. Accompanying him were the Twelve [2]and some women who had been cured of evil spirits and infirmities, Mary, called Magdalene, from whom seven demons had gone out, [3]Joanna, the wife of Herod's steward Chuza, Susanna, and many others who provided for them out of their resources.

The Parable of the Sower

[4]When a large crowd gathered, with people from one town after another journeying to him, he spoke in a parable. [5]"A sower went out to sow his seed. And as he sowed, some seed fell on the path and was trampled, and the birds of the sky ate it up. [6]Some seed fell on rocky ground, and when it grew, it withered for lack of moisture. [7]Some seed fell among thorns, and the thorns grew with it and choked it. [8]And some seed fell on good soil, and when it grew, it produced fruit a hundredfold." After saying this, he called out, "Whoever has ears to hear ought to hear."

The Purpose of the Parables

[9]Then his disciples asked him what the meaning of this parable might be. [10]He answered, "Knowledge of the mysteries of the kingdom of God has been granted to you; but to the rest, they are made known through parables so that 'they may look but not see, and hear but not understand.'

The Parable of the Sower Explained

[11]"This is the meaning of the parable. The seed is the word of God. [12]Those on the path are the ones who have heard, but the devil comes and takes away the word from their hearts that they may not believe and be saved. [13]Those on rocky ground are the ones who, when they hear, receive the word with joy, but they have no root; they

continue

8:1-3 Women disciples from Galilee

Jesus' ministry is sustained and supported by the resources of several wealthy women disciples; three are named here: Mary Magdalene, Joanna, and Susanna. Joanna's marriage to Herod's steward, Chuza, certainly raises speculation on how much Herod and his court would have known about Jesus.

Luke refers to Mary Magdalene as one "from whom seven demons had gone out" (v. 2). The longer ending of Mark is the only other place in the Gospel tradition that describes her similarly (Mark 16:9). Exactly what is meant by the "seven demons" is unclear. If Jesus performed an exorcism over Mary Magdalene, there is no record of it, save for these verses from Luke and Mark; "seven demons" heightens the severity of her earlier possession.

The other evangelists do not name the women disciples until the death account (see Matt 27:56; Mark 15:40; John 19:25). Because he names the women here, Luke, who avoids repetitions, does not identify them at the crucifixion scene. He does name Mary Magdalene and Joanna as witnesses to the resurrection, however (24:10).

This group of men and women will follow Jesus to Jerusalem and remain there through the resurrection, but only the women and some of the men will stand at the cross (23:49).

8:4-18 Parables and response

The parable of the sower and its explanation appear in all three Synoptics. Luke's rendition, as usual, is a more compact version of this familiar story, leaving out the detail about the scorching sun, the shallow depth of rocky soil, and the trampled path. While Matthew 13:2 and Mark 4:1 state that the large crowd forces Jesus to preach from a boat, Luke has Jesus standing in the boat earlier in the Gospel narrative (see 5:1-11). Luke also underscores that the people come to him "from one town after another" (v. 4); Jesus' reputation has spread.

In verses 9-10 Jesus offers an explanation for parables. The "mysteries of the kingdom" (v. 10) are most probably the intuitive knowledge that comes with the intimacy the disciples have with Jesus. Paradoxically, Jesus must still explain the parable to them. This explanation can also be a reference to Isaiah 6:9-10: "Listen carefully, but you shall not understand! / Look intently, but you shall know nothing!"

A **parable** is a short saying or story that provides a descriptive metaphor or analogy for the "kingdom of God" or imparts a moral perspective. Only Mark and Matthew have parable chapters, large collections of Jesus' parables joined together into one long discourse. Some of Jesus' best known parables, such as the Good Samaritan, the Prodigal Son, and Lazarus and the Rich Man, are found only in Luke (10:29-37; 15:11-32; 16:19-31).

That this parable is one of the clearest makes Jesus' commenting on it a puzzlement. Surely there are more difficult parables than this one that demand explanations. This dialogue, however, is the logical follow-up to the preceding one concerning the purpose of parables and an example of that intimacy the disciples have with the Lord. Its presence in the text most probably reflects the redaction of the early church in trying to underline the qualities of good disciples.

believe only for a time and fall away in time of trial. [14]As for the seed that fell among thorns, they are the ones who have heard, but as they go along, they are choked by the anxieties and riches and pleasures of life, and they fail to produce mature fruit. [15]But as for the seed that fell on rich soil, they are the ones who, when they have heard the word, embrace it with a generous and good heart, and bear fruit through perseverance.

The Parable of the Lamp

[16]"No one who lights a lamp conceals it with a vessel or sets it under a bed; rather, he places it on a lampstand so that those who enter may see the light. [17]For there is nothing hidden that will not become visible, and nothing secret that will not be known and come to light. [18]Take care, then, how you hear. To anyone who has, more will be given, and from the one who has not, even what he seems to have will be taken away."

continue

The term "seed" occurs six times in Matthew and Mark and four times in Luke. Most of the instances are in this parable and its explanation in all three Synoptics. Its use here and elsewhere shows that the word "seed" represents either the word of God or faith.

Naturally, among farmers the image is apt, and particularly so for Luke, who is writing for a community that tradition locates in Syria, one of the ancient world's breadbaskets. The farmers at this time would not plant the seed in rows as is done today; rather, they would walk along broadcasting the seed in front of them.

Any interpretation of this parable should allow for the fact that there is no limit given to the number of times the sower casts the seed. Just as a sower will go out at least once a year to plant, so will the word continue to fall on the soil. The emphasis in the parable is on the soil and the soil's response, not on the seed or the sower.

ates this theme when talking about the mustard seed (see Luke 13:19; 17:6).

Jesus and His Family

¹⁹Then his mother and his brothers came to him but were unable to join him because of the crowd. ²⁰He was told, "Your mother and your brothers are standing outside and they wish to see you." ²¹He said to them in reply, "My mother and my brothers are those who hear the word of God and act on it."

The Calming of a Storm at Sea

²²One day he got into a boat with his disciples and said to them, "Let us cross to the other side of the lake." So they set sail, ²³and while they were sailing he fell asleep. A squall blew over the lake, and they were taking in water and were in danger. ²⁴They came and woke him saying, "Master, master, we are perishing!" He awakened, rebuked the wind and the waves, and they subsided and there was a calm. ²⁵Then he asked them, "Where is your faith?" But they were filled with awe and amazed and said to one another, "Who then is this, who commands even the winds and the sea, and they obey him?"

continue

8:19-21 Jesus and his family

Luke is less harsh in recording this event than either of the other two synoptic writers. Jesus' mother and brothers are unable to reach him "because of the crowd." In the parallel accounts in Matthew and Mark, his mother and brothers come calling for him as if he were a family embarrassment.

The question of Jesus' brothers often arises, especially in the Catholic tradition, which holds that Jesus was the only child of Mary. Explanations that the Greek word for "brother," *adelphos*, can also mean "cousin" are not at all convincing. A better basis for the claim is also founded on tradition, which sees Joseph as a man older than the young woman Mary. This tradition holds that Joseph lost his first wife to childbirth, a death common for women throughout history. Jesus' brothers, then, are really Jesus' half-brothers from Joseph's first marriage. It is impossible to prove or disprove the details of Mary's perpetual virginity. Of course, the virginal conception of Jesus is not the issue under discussion here. Luke is explicit, as is Matthew, that when Mary was pregnant with Jesus, no human father was involved (see above, Luke 1:26-38).

This short passage redefines human relationships under Christ. At this time and place, the extended family was one's first and only locus of identification. To lose or be ostracized from the family was equivalent to losing all personhood. Jesus redefines the lines of association and kinship by broadening the family boundary. Now, the evangelist seems to say, disciples form a new family, which is all-inclusive of those who hear and do the word of God. These new bonds of relationship are developed in Luke's second volume, the Acts of the Apostles.

The connection that the parable of the lamp has with the explanation of the sower and the seed flows smoothly from Luke's hand. In a mixing of metaphors, the seed that has taken root in good soil now becomes a lamp. The knowledge of the mysteries of the kingdom, which we meet in verse 10, is catalyzed by the interpretation in verse 18: "To anyone who has, more will be given, and from the one who has not, even what he seems to have will be taken away." This verse is not describing the moral order; rather, it expresses growth in the word of God. Love and devotion to God build upon themselves and increase within a person to the point that others are drawn to God and the kingdom by the life of those who have let their seed flourish and their light shine. Jesus reiter-

8:22-25 The calming of the storm

With the phrase "One day" Luke shifts from Jesus' preaching to his performing miracles. The Lake of Galilee, below sea level and surrounded by hills and mountains, is well situated for sudden summer storms to arise without warning. As the hot, humid air rises, the colder air comes rushing in, causing large swells in a very small lake. Recent archaeological finds suggest that the boat would most likely have been between eight to nine meters in length (twenty-six to thirty feet), two to three meters wide (seven to nine feet), and about one to two meters high (four to six feet), certainly enough space for Jesus and a large group of disciples.

Although natural phenomena could explain the miracle—these storms subside almost as quickly as they arise—the miraculous lies at the juncture of human experience and divine intervention. People today still speak of a sudden prayer as saving them from a nearly fatal collision. There is no way to prove whether this event of calming the storm occurred or not. The believer would not be wrong to follow the tradition, which says that it did.

The importance of this story, however, is theological. Up until this point, Jesus has been ministering in the Jewish areas on the western and northern shores of the Sea of Galilee. When he says to his disciples, "Let us cross to the other side of the lake" (8:22), he means the eastern shore, which at that time was in the pagan district of the Decapolis, meaning "Ten Cities." Encountering a storm on the lake while heading toward pagan territory shows Jesus in a battle. He is taking on the cosmic forces arrayed against his ministry, and he will not be cowed by them. Here a storm, which in the pagan culture of the surrounding region would have been associated with the god Baal (see 1 Kgs 18), obeys Jesus' command and everyone is saved. He is the Lord of the cosmos.

The story ends with a question, "Who then is this . . ." (v. 25). Luke has been prompting us all along throughout this narrative with questions or statements concerning Jesus' identity (see 4:22, 34, 41; 5:21; 7:16, 49), and the evangelist will continue to do so (see 9:9) before Peter finally declares him to be the Messiah (9:20).

The Healing of the Gerasene Demoniac

[26]Then they sailed to the territory of the Gerasenes, which is opposite Galilee. [27]When he came ashore a man from the town who was possessed by demons met him. For a long time he had not worn clothes; he did not live in a house, but lived among the tombs. [28]When he saw Jesus, he cried out and fell down before him; in a loud voice he shouted, "What have you to do with me, Jesus, son of the Most High God? I beg you, do not torment me!" [29]For he had ordered the unclean spirit to come out of the man. (It had taken hold of him many times, and he used to be bound with chains and shackles as a restraint, but he would break his bonds and be driven by the demon into deserted places.) [30]Then Jesus asked him, "What is your name?" He replied, "Legion," because many demons had entered him. [31]And they pleaded with him not to order them to depart to the abyss.

continue

8:26-39 Exorcising the Gerasene demoniac

Having safely crossed the lake, Jesus and the disciples land on the eastern shore, in pagan territory. Immediately demonic forces again challenge Jesus' lordship, but this time from outside the Jewish districts.

All three Synoptics include this account of the Gerasene demoniac. The name of the locale has its textual problems. In the manuscript tradition, an alternate name for "Gerasene" is "Gadarene," a confusion stemming from the attempts of various scribes to harmonize all three accounts. This attempt at harmonization was further complicated by the fact that Matthew 8:28 reads "Gadarene." The names "Gerasene" and "Gadarene" are based on two separate cities in the Decapolis, Gerasa (or Jerash) and Gadara, respectively. Neither is located on the Sea of Galilee, although Gadara is closer to the lake than Gerasa. Most likely each city's name was used interchangeably as

³²A herd of many swine was feeding there on the hillside, and they pleaded with him to allow them to enter those swine; and he let them. ³³The demons came out of the man and entered the swine, and the herd rushed down the steep bank into the lake and was drowned. ³⁴When the swineherds saw what had happened, they ran away and reported the incident in the town and throughout the countryside. ³⁵People came out to see what had happened and, when they approached Jesus, they discovered the man from whom the demons had come out sitting at his feet. He was clothed and in his right mind, and they were seized with fear. ³⁶Those who witnessed it told them how the possessed man had been saved. ³⁷The entire population of the region of the Gerasenes asked Jesus to leave them because they were seized with great fear. So he got into a boat and returned. ³⁸The man from whom the demons had come out begged to remain with him, but he sent him away, saying, ³⁹"Return home and recount what God has done for you." The man went off and proclaimed throughout the whole town what Jesus had done for him.

continue

is to exercise control, and the demons freely give it, recognizing that they must be obedient to him. Luke alone states that the demons beg not to be sent to the abyss (v. 31). The swine, impure animals to the Jews, represent the demons' own uncleanness. In biblical Jewish thought, large bodies of water symbolized the entrance to the abyss, or Sheol. In his exorcism, Jesus sends the demons back to where they come from, the dwelling of the dead. On the one hand, he countermands their wish, and on the other, he proves to all that the demons had actually left the individual.

The pagan man, now free of demons, but bereft of friends and family due to his former state, wants to follow Jesus (v. 38). Jesus turns him into a Gentile missionary going through the city (Gadara? Gerasa?). Thus Luke prepares the reader for the mission to the Gentiles, a major theme in the Acts of the Apostles.

In Luke's narrative of Jesus' earthly ministry, Jesus has been battling the diabolical forces in the world ever since his temptation in the desert. The victory he has with this demoniac functions simultaneously as a realization and as an anticipation of the eschaton. In the former, all witness the flight of a legion of evil spirits. Yet the decisive showdown with Satan has yet to occur, and it will not come until Jesus dies and rises in Jerusalem.

the generic term for the area on the eastern shore, and exacting scribes, trying to address the discrepancies in the text, actually caused more confusion. The tradition locates the site at Kursi, in the northeast quadrant of the Sea of Galilee, which sits on a steep hill above the shoreline.

Not only is the man a demoniac but also, since he lives in tombs, he would be ritually impure to the religious Jews. He calls out to Jesus in a "loud voice" (v. 28), a signal of impending judgment. Unlike Matthew or Mark, Luke notes that Jesus had commanded the spirit to depart from the man even before the demoniac speaks.

Jesus demands the demons' name in order to show his authority over them, although he uses the singular of the noun. To know a name

Location of Mount Tabor

8:40-56 Jairus's daughter and the woman with a hemorrhage

Luke follows Mark's order of having one miracle, the hemorrhaging woman, surrounded by another, the raising of Jairus's daughter.

Verse 40 informs us that Jesus has returned to the Jewish districts on the western shore of the Sea of Galilee. Luke, always the evangelist to find joy in the Gospel, specifies that the crowd "welcomed" Jesus. At this point the story of Jairus's daughter is introduced. Verse 42 prepares us for the resolution of the story, when the hemorrhaging woman enters the picture in the next verse and turns our attention.

The woman touches the tassel on Jesus' cloak (v. 44). The term "tassel" most likely refers to the fringes religious Jewish men were commanded to wear on the corners of their outer garment in Numbers 15:38. The Greek Old Testament, or Septuagint, calls these tassels *kraspedon*, the same word Luke employs here. The woman is not merely grabbing at Jesus; she wants to clutch the holiest part of his clothing, a sign of her faith. Fearing rebuke, she falls at Jesus' feet. She bears witness to Jesus' miraculous act in front of all (v. 47), while Jesus commends and blesses her. Her faith opened her to Jesus' cure (v. 48).

Luke keeps the narrative flowing by having a messenger arrive from Jairus's house with the news that the young girl is dead (v. 49) even as Jesus is still speaking. When Jesus states that Jairus' daughter is only sleeping, this crowd, different from the one that initially welcomed Jesus, ridicules him. The comparison between the people in the two groups is noteworthy. The first, not enveloped by the fear and dread of losing a child, are in better straits to receive Jesus and his message with happiness and joy. The second, however, watching the passing of the girl and seeing the suffering of the parents, are too preoccupied to concern themselves with Jesus' visit. The Lord's visitation, however, comes to them, too, with the resuscitation of the daughter. Once again, faith is the operative condition for this miracle (v. 50).

Jesus allows only Peter, John, and James to enter the house with him. These three are

Jairus's Daughter and the Woman with a Hemorrhage

[40]When Jesus returned, the crowd welcomed him, for they were all waiting for him. [41]And a man named Jairus, an official of the synagogue, came forward. He fell at the feet of Jesus and begged him to come to his house, [42]because he had an only daughter, about twelve years old, and she was dying. As he went, the crowds almost crushed him. [43]And a woman afflicted with hemorrhages for twelve years, who [had spent her whole livelihood on doctors and] was unable to be cured by anyone, [44]came up behind him and touched the tassel on his cloak. Immediately her bleeding stopped. [45]Jesus then asked, "Who touched me?" While all were denying it, Peter said, "Master, the crowds are pushing and pressing in upon you." [46]But Jesus said, "Someone has touched me; for I know that power has gone out from me." [47]When the woman realized that she had not escaped notice, she came forward trembling. Falling down before him, she explained in the presence of all the people why she had touched him and how she had been healed immediately. [48]He said to her, "Daughter, your faith has saved you; go in peace."

[49]While he was still speaking, someone from the synagogue official's house arrived and said, "Your daughter is dead; do not trouble the teacher any longer." [50]On hearing this, Jesus answered him, "Do not be afraid; just have faith and she will be saved." [51]When he arrived at the house he allowed no one to enter with him except Peter and John and James, and the child's father and mother. [52]All were weeping and mourning for her, when he said, "Do not weep any longer, for she is not dead, but sleeping." [53]And they ridiculed him, because they knew that she was dead. [54]But he took her by the hand and called to her, "Child, arise!" [55]Her breath returned and she immediately arose. He then directed that she should be given something to eat. [56]Her parents were astounded, and he instructed them to tell no one what had happened.

continue

CHAPTER 9

The Mission of the Twelve

[1]He summoned the Twelve and gave them power and authority over all demons and to cure diseases, [2]and he sent them to proclaim the kingdom of God and to heal [the sick]. [3]He said to them, "Take nothing for the journey, neither walking stick, nor sack, nor food, nor money, and let no one take a second tunic. [4]Whatever house you enter, stay there and leave from there. [5]And as for those who do not welcome you, when you leave that town, shake the dust from your feet in testimony against them." [6]Then they set out and went from village to village proclaiming the good news and curing diseases everywhere.

Herod's Opinion of Jesus

[7]Herod the tetrarch heard about all that was happening, and he was greatly perplexed because some were saying, "John has been raised from the dead"; [8]others were saying, "Elijah has appeared"; still others, "One of the ancient prophets has arisen." [9]But Herod said, "John I beheaded. Who then is this about whom I hear such things?" And he kept trying to see him.

The Return of the Twelve and the Feeding of the Five Thousand

[10]When the apostles returned, they explained to him what they had done. He took them and withdrew in private to a town called Bethsaida. [11]The crowds, meanwhile, learned of this and followed him. He received them and spoke to them about the kingdom of God, and he healed those who needed to be cured. [12]As the day was drawing to a close, the Twelve approached him and said, "Dismiss the crowd so that they can go to the surrounding villages and farms and find lodging and provisions; for we are in a deserted place here." [13]He said to them, "Give them some food yourselves." They replied, "Five loaves and two fish are all we have, unless we ourselves go and buy food for all these people." [14]Now the men

continue

selected out from the other members of the Twelve at the transfiguration as well (9:28). Peter occupies a central role in the Acts of the Apostles and the early church. John and James are the sons of Zebedee (5:10); the latter was martyred by Herod Agrippa (Acts 12:2), but what of John? There is a tradition that he is the Beloved Disciple, the author of the Fourth Gospel (John 13:23; 19:26; 20:2; 21:7, 20-24), but this conclusion cannot be substantiated with absolute certainty. Nonetheless, Paul refers to James, John, and Peter (Kephas) as "pillars" of the church in Jerusalem (Gal 2:9).

9:1-6 The mission of the Twelve

The ninth chapter of Luke introduces a shift in focus. Whereas Luke treats the Galilean ministry in chapters 4 through 8, chapter 9 turns the narrative's attention to the disciples and the beginning of the journey to Jerusalem.

By giving the Twelve authority over the demons, and linking that with the kingdom of God and curing, Luke heightens the eschatological tone of Jesus' ministry. Jesus empowers his followers to join the cosmic battle with Satan. This warfare begins in the temptation scene (Luke 4:1-13) and surfaces throughout the Gospel, coming to a head at the crucifixion.

The injunction to take nothing for the journey ensures complete trust in God. That the Twelve are successful in their curing demonstrates that the kingdom of God has arrived. While this passage is most likely describing the missionary activity of the early church, it does not discount the probability that Jesus had at least the Twelve performing similar deeds in his life on earth. The parallels in the other Synoptics support such an assertion.

The Twelve are commissioned and sent (*apostellō*, 6:2), from which we get the word "apostle." On their names, see Luke 6:12-16.

9:7-9 Herod's thoughts

Herod Antipas was tetrarch of Galilee and Perea. His query in verse 9 echoes that of the disciples in the storm-tossed boat in Luke 8:25

and gives the reader an idea of the questions circulating during Christianity's infancy: Who is Jesus, and, in this case, what is his relationship to John the Baptist? In the Jewish tradition, Elijah is supposed to return to usher in the messianic age. See also 23:6-12.

Herod's wily and suspicious nature comes through in this passage. Unlike Matthew and Mark, Luke does not report Herod's infamous birthday celebration, which leads to the beheading of the Baptist, although earlier in his Gospel the third evangelist notifies the reader that Herod has had John imprisoned (3:19-20). From the Jewish historian Josephus (*Ant.* 18.5.2), we obtain the information that Herod put John to death at his fortress-palace of Machaerus in the Transjordan.

In this description, Josephus also mentions the important detail that Herod feared John because the Baptist drew large crowds. Crowds could always fall into rioting and insurrection. Eventually both Roman and Jewish authorities will have similar fear of Jesus and will form an alliance to execute him as well.

9:10-17 Return of the Twelve and the feeding of the five thousand

Luke, as well as Mark, juxtaposes the return of the apostles with Herod's questioning about Jesus' identity. Herod tries to suppress the movement even as the movement continues to grow despite his efforts. Bethsaida, a town east of the Jordan River but on the northern shore of the Sea of Galilee, is part of the "Gospel Triangle," that segment of the land about which nearly eighty percent of Jesus' ministry takes place. Just south of the town lies a volcanic deposit of basalt rock and rubble making farming or habitation impossible. Most likely this locale is the "private" area mentioned in verse 10.

The account of the feeding of the five thousand occurs in all four Gospels, though Matthew 15:32-39 and Mark 8:1-10 also feature a feeding of four thousand. The action of first blessing and then breaking the bread has

there numbered about five thousand. Then he said to his disciples, "Have them sit down in groups of [about] fifty." [15]They did so and made them all sit down. [16]Then taking the five loaves and the two fish, and looking up to heaven, he said the blessing over them, broke them, and gave them to the disciples to set before the crowd. [17]They all ate and were satisfied. And when the leftover fragments were picked up, they filled twelve wicker baskets.

continue

strong eucharistic overtones, and as such, provides eschatological imagery.

Other details play into this imagery as well. Fish, because of their abundance, often symbolize the eschatological banquet. They can also refer to *garum*, a relish made of putrefying fish that was in heavy demand throughout the ancient Mediterranean world. The Greek verb *kataklinō* in verse 14 means to sit or recline at dinner, another reference to the eschatological banquet.

Luke has the crowd gather specifically in groups of fifty, which divides into five thousand evenly. Such a refinement allows Pentecost to function as an interpretive backdrop. In the Jewish tradition at this time, Pentecost was a celebration of the grain harvest and took place fifty days or seven weeks after Passover. In time the feast came to celebrate the giving of the Law to Moses, but whether it commemorated the Sinai covenant at this period is difficult to determine. In any case, the abundance of grain at harvest time symbolizes the abundant blessing of the end times. That five loaves of bread plus two fish equal the number seven underscores the emphasis on Pentecost. Of course, Luke writes about Pentecost in Acts 2, and that feast has prime importance in his work. The feeding of the five thousand, therefore, is one of Luke's ways to foreshadow the eschaton.

Peter's Confession about Jesus

[18]Once when Jesus was praying in solitude, and the disciples were with him, he asked them, "Who do the crowds say that I am?" [19]They said in reply, "John the Baptist; others, Elijah; still others, 'One of the ancient prophets has arisen.'" [20]Then he said to them, "But who do you say that I am?" Peter said in reply, "The Messiah of God." [21]He rebuked them and directed them not to tell this to anyone.

The First Prediction of the Passion

[22]He said, "The Son of Man must suffer greatly and be rejected by the elders, the chief priests, and the scribes, and be killed and on the third day be raised."

The Conditions of Discipleship

[23]Then he said to all, "If anyone wishes to come after me, he must deny himself and take up his cross daily and follow me. [24]For whoever wishes to save his life will lose it, but whoever loses his life for my sake will save it. [25]What profit is there for one to gain the whole world yet lose or forfeit himself? [26]Whoever is ashamed of me and of my words, the Son of Man will be ashamed of when he comes in his glory and in the glory of the Father and of the holy angels. [27]Truly I say to you, there are some standing here who will not taste death until they see the kingdom of God."

The Transfiguration of Jesus

[28]About eight days after he said this, he took Peter, John, and James and went up the mountain to pray. [29]While he was praying his face changed in appearance and his clothing became dazzling white. [30]And behold, two men were conversing with him, Moses and Elijah, [31]who appeared in glory and spoke of his exodus that he was going to accomplish in Jerusalem. [32]Peter and his companions had been overcome by sleep, but becoming fully awake, they saw his glory and the two men standing with him. [33]As they were about to part from him, Peter said to Jesus, "Master, it is

continue

9:18-27 Peter's confession and the cost of discipleship

Luke is the only evangelist to open Peter's confession scene with Jesus at prayer. Although Matthew has the most elaborate version of Peter's confession, the other synoptic writers recount it. In all three Gospels, Jesus poses the question to the disciples, but Peter is the only one who answers. Their comments about John the Baptist and Elijah recapitulate Herod's thoughts in trying to identify Jesus. Elijah was the prophet whose return would usher in the coming of the Messiah. John the Baptist, as precursor, fits into this category as well, and mention of his name here reflects the early Christian community's appeal to the Baptist's disciples, who still feel that the Baptist is the Messiah.

All Synoptics display a set of three passion predictions. This one is Luke's first (see 9:44; 18:31-33). The context colors the moment. The eschatological overtones in both the feeding of the five thousand and Peter's confession take on a stark reality in the passion prediction. Yes, Jesus is the Messiah ushering in a new age in which all can participate, but that new age comes with a price.

An aphorism encapsulates one of the great paradoxes of Christian life: gain is really loss and loss is really gain (v. 24). In the Lukan narrative, these words prepare the disciples for what lies ahead as it encourages the Lukan community. The eschatological term "Son of Man," along with one of Luke's favorite phrases, "kingdom of God," reaffirms the eschatological dimension that must be a part of any disciple of Christ.

9:28-36 The transfiguration of Jesus

Chapter 9 continues to focus on the small group of disciples, and once again we see Jesus at prayer. The interplay between the mission, eschatological feeding, confession, passion prediction, conditions of discipleship, and now transfiguration form a synthesis of Christian life.

What is the purpose of following Jesus, and where will it all lead? Luke as well as Matthew and Mark answers the question with the transfiguration. Many consider this event to be an account of a post-resurrection appearance. That all three Synoptics situate it within the ministry, however, militates against such an interpretation. It is better to view it as a foreshadowing of the glorification of the resurrection. Placed within this context of passion predictions and discipleship, the transfigured Christ shows the disciples, through Peter, James, and John, the promise that discipleship can bring both to this life and the life to come.

Moses and Elijah, representing the Law and the Prophets, respectively, give their approbation to what the disciples are seeing. Elijah's presence also has an element of foreshadowing; according to Jewish tradition, he is to usher in the messianic age. Both these worthies speak to Jesus of the "exodus" he is about to accomplish in Jerusalem (v. 31). "Exodus" has a double meaning. Naturally, the reader draws on the account of the Israelites' deliverance from death and slavery in Egypt to freedom and new life in the Promised Land. "Exodus," however, can also refer to death. On this basis, Jesus' death is a deliverance from slavery to new life, and his exodus is completed at the resurrection and ascension. Because so much of the material in this chapter deals with discipleship, the meaning death has for Jesus is the same for those who follow him.

The voice from the cloud resonates with the voice at the baptism (3:21-22), but with two differences. At the baptism, Luke writes, the voice comes from heaven and says, "You are my beloved Son; with you I am well pleased"; but here at the transfiguration, the voice comes from the cloud and says, "This is my chosen Son; listen to him" (v. 35). Because the voice from heaven at the baptism is in the second person, only Jesus hears it. At the transfiguration, the voice is in the third person, allowing the three disciples to hear it as well. The reference to the cloud is an echo from Exodus, where the glory of God's presence (Shekinah) is depicted as a cloud (Exod 13:21). God is present at the transfiguration too.

In Matthew's and Mark's versions of the transfiguration, Jesus commands the three disciples not to say anything about what they had

good that we are here; let us make three tents, one for you, one for Moses, and one for Elijah." But he did not know what he was saying. [34]While he was still speaking, a cloud came and cast a shadow over them, and they became frightened when they entered the cloud. [35]Then from the cloud came a voice that said, "This is my chosen Son; listen to him." [36]After the voice had spoken, Jesus was found alone. They fell silent and did not at that time tell anyone what they had seen.

The Healing of a Boy with a Demon

[37]On the next day, when they came down from the mountain, a large crowd met him. [38]There was a man in the crowd who cried out, "Teacher, I beg you, look at my son; he is my only child. [39]For a spirit seizes him and he suddenly screams and it convulses him until he foams at the mouth; it releases him only with difficulty, wearing him out.

continue

seen. Luke simply writes, however, that the three kept silent about the whole event "at that time" (v. 36). Although noting that the place of the transfiguration was of no importance to Luke, the tradition, based on Matthew 17:1 and Mark 9:2, locates it on Mount Tabor.

Placed in the context of the mission, eschatology, passion, and discipleship, the transfiguration becomes part of the promise to those who follow Jesus. As he is transfigured into glory by following the Father's will, so too will each Christian disciple be transfigured.

9:37-50 Exorcism and lessons on the kingdom

This case of demonic possession balances the eschatological tone of transfigured glorification by interjecting an attack from the realm of evil. Though the boy's symptoms seem like a case of epilepsy, and may very well have been, sickness was often attributed to the machinations of the devil. In the sense that goodness is from God and illness is not a good, the ancient

⁴⁰I begged your disciples to cast it out but they could not." ⁴¹Jesus said in reply, "O faithless and perverse generation, how long will I be with you and endure you? Bring your son here." ⁴²As he was coming forward, the demon threw him to the ground in a convulsion; but Jesus rebuked the unclean spirit, healed the boy, and returned him to his father. ⁴³And all were astonished by the majesty of God.

The Second Prediction of the Passion

While they were all amazed at his every deed, he said to his disciples, ⁴⁴"Pay attention to what I am telling you. The Son of Man is to be handed over to men." ⁴⁵But they did not understand this saying; its meaning was hidden from them so that they should not understand it, and they were afraid to ask him about this saying.

The Greatest in the Kingdom

⁴⁶An argument arose among the disciples about which of them was the greatest. ⁴⁷Jesus realized the intention of their hearts and took a child and placed it by his side ⁴⁸and said to them, "Whoever receives this child in my name receives me, and whoever receives me receives the one who sent me. For the one who is least among all of you is the one who is the greatest."

Another Exorcist

⁴⁹Then John said in reply, "Master, we saw someone casting out demons in your name and we tried to prevent him because he does not follow in our company." ⁵⁰Jesus said to him, "Do not prevent him, for whoever is not against you is for you."

interpretation hits the mark. Jesus, the one whom Peter confesses as the Messiah and the one whose glory is seen in the transfiguration, reclaims creation for God in the cure of the possessed boy. Only Luke concludes this story by saying that all were "astonished by the majesty of God" (v. 43). Not only does this bit of editing

direct attention to the true source and goal of the exorcism, but it also enables the evangelist to omit verses that underscore the disciples' poor performance (see Matt 17:19-20; Mark 9:28-29). In his harsh words, Jesus shows his frustration in getting the message across to those closest to him (v. 41).

While all are marveling at God's greatness, Jesus predicts his passion for the second time (vv. 45-46). The redemption of creation will not be easy and will not be without suffering and death, a sober reminder after the transfiguration and the exorcism. The Lukan Jesus is emphatic about the suffering he must undergo (v. 44). Matthew and Mark do not include this heightened urgency in their parallel accounts. All three Synoptics, however, show the disciples afraid to ask for clarification about the upcoming passion. Luke states that the meaning was "hidden" from them (v. 45), a comment that ties into Jesus' frustration at verse 41 and leads into the instruction on greatness.

The disciples have difficulty comprehending the meaning behind the life and work of Jesus, as the argument about greatness demonstrates (vv. 46-48). With all they have seen in the ministry, all they have experienced by way of miracles, healings, and for at least three of them, the transfiguration, they still measure success according to the world's standards. The child whom Jesus placed at his side was most probably part of a group of children who would beg, pester, and tag along with these strangers for part of the distance through a town. Receiving a child like this is not always easy to do, yet that is the point of Jesus' action. Furthermore, in the society of that time, children were obligated to show respect to adults, not vice versa. The placement of this pericope after the second passion prediction for a lesson on greatness is particularly apropos.

The account about another exorcist (vv. 49-50) highlights the dispute about prestige and the rivalry the disciples have among themselves. The jealousies of the petty despots who ruled all of Palestine often prevented them from working toward mutual self-interest. For the Christian, the horizon line must be higher.

EXPLORING LESSON FIVE

1. What did the women who accompanied Jesus and his disciples contribute to his mission (8:1-3)? (See 23:49; 24:10; Matt 27:56; Mark 15:40; John 19:25.)

_____

_____

_____

_____

_____

2. a) When have you experienced the power of the seed (the word of God) springing up and bearing fruit in your life (8:4-15)?

_____

_____

_____

   b) When has the soil of your life not been so conducive for the seeds' growth?

_____

_____

_____

3. Given the cultural context of the times, how would Jesus' message concerning who belonged in his family have been revolutionary (8:19-21)?

_____

_____

_____

_____

_____

4. How does knowing something about the culture of the region found "opposite Galilee" bring added insights into the account of the Gerasene demoniac (8:26-39)? (See Matt 4:15.)

_____

_____

_____

_____

_____

5. The hemorrhaging woman and Jairus each approach Jesus with expectation and hope (8:40-56). Can you recall a time when you reached out to Jesus in this way? What was the result?

_____

_____

_____

_____

_____

6. Jesus sends the Twelve out to be extensions of his own ministry of proclaiming the kingdom of God (9:1-6) and later describes the obligations of discipleship (9:23-27). In what ways have you answered a call to proclaim the Good News of God's kingdom? What sacrifices has that required of you?

_____

_____

_____

_____

_____

7. In several places in this lesson, the importance of naming who Jesus is has been introduced. These include when he calms the storm (8:22-25), when he asks the disciples who both the crowds and they themselves say he is (9:18-21), and elsewhere (9:7-9). How do your life and your words confess who Jesus is to you? How has such a confession of faith in who Jesus is been significant in your life?

_____

_____

_____

_____

_____

8. What are some "eucharistic overtones" found in Luke's account of the feeding of the five thousand (9:10-17)? (See 22:19; 24:30.)

_____

_____

_____

_____

_____

9. How does Luke tie Jesus' transfiguration to God's previous saving deeds in the Old
   Testament and to the passion that awaits Jesus in Jerusalem (9:28-36)?

_____

_____

_____

_____

_____

_____

10. What ecumenical implications (relations between Catholics and non-Catholics) do you see
    in Luke 9:49-50?

_____

_____

_____

_____

_____

_____

See next page for closing prayer.

CLOSING PRAYER

Prayer

"If anyone wishes to come after me, he must deny himself and take up his cross daily and follow me." (Luke 9:23)

Jesus, as you turn toward Jerusalem, you invite us to accompany you. It is a road that teaches self-denial and equips us to carry our crosses. We pray for strength and courage, but we also pray for the joy that comes from following in your footsteps. Give us courage in these areas . . .

LESSON SIX

Luke 9:51–11:54

Begin your personal study and group discussion with a simple and sincere prayer such as:

Prayer

O God of Joy, send your Spirit with a freshness that will help me hear familiar words with open ears and heart. Guide me as I pray and study the Gospel of Luke.

Read the Bible text of Luke 9:51–11:54, found in the outside columns of pages 82–93, highlighting what stands out to you.

Read the accompanying commentary to add to your understanding.

Respond to the questions on pages 94–96, Exploring Lesson Six.

The closing prayer on page 97 is for your personal use and may be used at the end of group discussion.

V: The Journey to Jerusalem: Luke's Travel Narrative

Departure for Jerusalem; Samaritan Inhospitality

[51]When the days for his being taken up were fulfilled, he resolutely determined to journey to Jerusalem, [52]and he sent messengers ahead of him. On the way they entered a Samaritan village to prepare for his reception there, [53]but they would not welcome him because the destination of his journey was Jerusalem. [54]When the disciples James and John saw this they asked, "Lord, do you want us to call down fire from heaven to consume them?" [55]Jesus turned and rebuked them, [56]and they journeyed to another village.

The Would-be Followers of Jesus

[57]As they were proceeding on their journey someone said to him, "I will follow you wherever you go." [58]Jesus answered him, "Foxes have dens and birds of the sky have nests, but the Son of Man has nowhere to rest his head." [59]And to another he said, "Follow me." But he replied, "[Lord,] let me go first and bury my father." [60]But he answered him, "Let the dead bury their dead. But you, go and proclaim the kingdom of God." [61]And another said, "I will follow you, Lord, but first let me say farewell to my family at home." [62][To him] Jesus said, "No one who sets a hand to the plow and looks to what was left behind is fit for the kingdom of God."

continue

THE JOURNEY TO JERUSALEM

Luke 9:51–19:27

In all three Synoptic accounts, Jesus makes only one trip to Jerusalem, and that journey ends in his passion, death, and resurrection. Luke is the only evangelist, however, to magnify Jerusalem's theological purpose; it is the crucible into which Jesus' whole earthly ministry is funneled. Jerusalem becomes the city of destiny.

This point also marks the beginning of what some scholars call the "Big Interpolation," a large section of material that cannot be linked to Mark and, with few exceptions, has no parallel in Q. The interpolation extends to 18:14.

9:51-56 Departure for Jerusalem and Samaritan inhospitality

Luke describes the shift toward the holy city most dramatically (v. 51). The phrase "When the days for being taken up were fulfilled" signals the end of his Galilean ministry according to a divine plan. "He resolutely determined to journey to Jerusalem" shows an intensity of purpose in completing that divine plan. Luke's vocabulary in verse 51 breathes with metaphor. The Greek for "being taken up, received up" is the word *analēmpsis*, which means both "ascension" and "death." When combined with the "exodus" referred to in the transfiguration (v. 31), there develops the composite picture of death and glorification.

Jesus is going up, both literally and figuratively. Jerusalem is over 900 meters (2700 feet) above sea level, while the Sea of Galilee is nearly 100 meters (300 feet) below; he and his disciples must climb the Judean mountains to reach the city. Metaphorically, after the passion, death, and resurrection, Jesus will ascend to the Father, an ascension that also is his glorification. These events begin and, in a large way, take place within the time frame of Passover, the Jewish commemoration of the Exodus.

Luke's detail about passing through the Samaritan villages raises some questions. Jews in Galilee would avoid passing through Samaria as they made their way south to Jerusalem. The usual route was to walk along the Jordan Valley and begin the ascent at Jericho. It appears that Luke might be relying on some ancient tradition that Jesus passed through, if not ministered in, Samaria. John's story of the Samaritan woman at the well (4:4-41) corroborates Jesus' presence in that territory. Moreover, according to Acts, Samaria was the first non-Jewish region to be converted to Christianity. This short foray into Samaria functions as a foreshadowing of the missionary activity that the Acts of the Apostles will detail. Jesus' rebuke constitutes his stand against vengeance and violence, as well as reflecting his attitude toward missionary activity (see 9:5).

9:57-62 Would-be followers of Jesus

Whereas the disciples have already heard the discourse on the cost of discipleship (see 9:23-27), others joining Jesus have not. Jesus relates the proper comportment in three situations: one to a person who is ready to give all for the kingdom, another to a person who is asked to give all for the kingdom, and still another to one who wants to hold back from giving all to the kingdom. Jesus challenges them by using imagery and hyperbole. The curt answers he gives show the rhythm of someone hurrying with a direct purpose in mind, and the vacillation Jesus encounters with these three would deflect from that purpose.

To the first individual, Jesus underscores that personal comfort will often have to give way to the demands of discipleship. His response to the second may seem harsh, but in no way is it to be understood as negating one's obligations to one's parents or family. Rather, Jesus is seeing through what constitutes a lame excuse while speaking on a symbolic level. To follow Jesus is to enter into a life-giving relationship. There are plenty of people who refuse this relationship, and in this sense they are

CHAPTER 10

The Mission of the Seventy-two

[1]After this the Lord appointed seventy [-two] others whom he sent ahead of him in pairs to every town and place he intended to visit. [2]He said to them, "The harvest is abundant but the laborers are few; so ask the master of the harvest to send out laborers for his harvest. [3]Go on your way; behold, I am sending you like lambs among wolves. [4]Carry no money bag, no sack, no sandals; and greet no one along the way. [5]Into whatever house you enter, first say, 'Peace to this household.' [6]If a peaceful person lives there, your peace will rest on him; but if not, it will return to you. [7]Stay in the same house and eat and drink what is offered to you, for the laborer deserves his payment. Do not move about from one house to another.

continue

dead; they can bury the physically dead. The reply to the third individual likewise shows the immediacy of the call. In the Jewish and Hellenistic societies, family bonds were very tight and could hold one back from being a disciple. Jesus first addresses this situation in 8:19-21, and his answer here is similar.

10:1-16 The mission of the seventy-two

The ancient manuscripts are evenly divided over whether the mission involves seventy or seventy-two disciples. Both numbers have a basis in the Old Testament. Seventy-two is a multiple of twelve, the number of the tribes of Israel; thus, by their going forth, a like number of disciples could represent the universalism of Jesus' mission. Alternatively, the narrative in Exodus 24 includes seventy elders who ascend the mountain with Moses, thereby making the disciples representatives of the Mosaic tradition.

Luke is the only evangelist to have a commissioning of a second group. In comparing the directives to the seventy-two disciples with

⁸Whatever town you enter and they welcome you, eat what is set before you, ⁹cure the sick in it and say to them, 'The kingdom of God is at hand for you.' ¹⁰Whatever town you enter and they do not receive you, go out into the streets and say, ¹¹'The dust of your town that clings to our feet, even that we shake off against you.' Yet know this: the kingdom of God is at hand. ¹²I tell you, it will be more tolerable for Sodom on that day than for that town.

Reproaches to Unrepentant Towns

¹³"Woe to you, Chorazin! Woe to you, Bethsaida! For if the mighty deeds done in your midst had been done in Tyre and Sidon, they would long ago have repented, sitting in sackcloth and ashes. ¹⁴But it will be more tolerable for Tyre and Sidon at the judgment than for you. ¹⁵And as for you, Capernaum, 'Will you be exalted to heaven? You will go down to the netherworld.'" ¹⁶Whoever listens to you listens to me. Whoever rejects you rejects me. And whoever rejects me rejects the one who sent me."

Return of the Seventy-two

¹⁷The seventy [-two] returned rejoicing, and said, "Lord, even the demons are subject to us because of your name." ¹⁸Jesus said, "I have observed Satan fall like lightning from the sky. ¹⁹Behold, I have given you the power 'to tread upon serpents' and scorpions and upon the full force of the enemy and nothing will harm you. ²⁰Nevertheless, do not rejoice because the spirits are subject to you, but rejoice because your names are written in heaven."

continue

the commissioning of the Twelve (9:1-6), we can see some differences as well as some points of contact. The Twelve are given authority over demons and the ability to cure diseases. Furthermore, they are charged with proclaiming the good news. The seventy-two disciples, on the other hand, travel in pairs as they bring the good news to households and towns. They are told to cure the sick, but Jesus says nothing about exorcizing demons; yet, they also do so (see v. 17).

Both the Twelve and the seventy-two are to travel light and perform with a singularity of purpose. In this section Jesus calls attention to attributes of Middle Eastern hospitality: there will always be someone to invite them into his or her home. The seventy-two are also told not to abuse the hospitality shown them (v. 8). Both groups are to shake the dust from the street of those towns that do not accept them (v. 11). An important difference, however, is that the seventy-two are to go ahead of Jesus and prepare towns for Jesus' eventual visit.

There is much debate on who constitutes the seventy-two. Were the Twelve selected from the seventy-two, or did they stand independent of them? Were there only seventy-two disciples, or were these seventy-two chosen from a much larger group? Were women in the line of Deborah, Hulda, Esther, Miriam, and Ruth involved, or was the mission restricted to men? These questions are difficult to answer. The important point is that Jesus commissions others to do his work on earth, and as such, the church does that work in him and in his name. Indeed, like the seventy-two, the church prepares the world for Jesus' visitation.

Jesus' comment about Sodom places the Christian message in context. To refuse the redemption he offers is a more heinous sin than any transgressions of sexual morality or proper hospitality. Even the Gentile cities of Tyre and Sidon will fare better, since they can read the signs of the times (v. 13).

10:17-20 Return of the seventy-two

The joy of the seventy-two disciples arises from the power they have over demons, a power given them by Jesus and only in his name. Jesus' response in verse 18 seems awkward to many. Some scholars have suggested that the proper translation should be "They have observed Satan fall like lightning from the sky," with the subject of the imperfect verb, *theōreō* ("observe"), being "demons" in verse

17. Greek grammar can support such a construction. A conclusion can be that since the demons see Satan fall from the sky, they easily submit to the disciples. The disciples, empowered by Jesus, become agents with him in furthering the realm of God.

The section closes with Jesus reaffirming the purpose and direction of the disciples' new power. They are not self-serving magicians or sorcerers; they are participants in Jesus' ministry. The disciples, like Jesus and those whom they help, find their reward in God, a point that gains in importance as they follow him to the cross in Jerusalem.

10:21-24 The prayer of Jesus and blessing of the disciples

Luke frequently shows Jesus at prayer. Reflecting the joy the disciples display in their return, Jesus offers praise and thanksgiving to the Father. Luke connects this joy to the Spirit, who, in the Acts of the Apostles, takes on a greater role of consoling and fructifying (see Acts 2:1-36). Luke's reversal theme is evident in verse 21, with revelation coming to the childlike but not to the wise and learned. The whole monologue appears to come from Q (see Matt 11:25-27; 13:16-17) and is one of the few places in the synoptic tradition that shows Jesus explaining his relationship to the Father in a pattern that seems very Johannine.

The disciples, who went out on the mission without money bag, sack, or sandals, receive a great reward in their experience of life in the Lord. The prophets and kings did not see or hear the Messiah of God (Luke 9:20), but the disciples have seen and heard not only the Messiah but also the works done in his name. These works consist in redeeming the world from Satan's clutches.

10:25-29 The greatest commandment

Jesus answers the "scholar of the law" or lawyer with a question. This tack precludes any trap or misunderstanding by unveiling the true motivation on the lawyer's part. The verb "test" in verse 25 is also applied to the devil in the temptation scene (Luke 4:12), thereby em-

Praise of the Father

²¹At that very moment he rejoiced [in] the holy Spirit and said, "I give you praise, Father, Lord of heaven and earth, for although you have hidden these things from the wise and the learned you have revealed them to the childlike. Yes, Father, such has been your gracious will. ²²All things have been handed over to me by my Father. No one knows who the Son is except the Father, and who the Father is except the Son and anyone to whom the Son wishes to reveal him."

The Privileges of Discipleship

²³Turning to the disciples in private he said, "Blessed are the eyes that see what you see. ²⁴For I say to you, many prophets and kings desired to see what you see, but did not see it, and to hear what you hear, but did not hear it."

The Greatest Commandment

²⁵There was a scholar of the law who stood up to test him and said, "Teacher, what must I do to inherit eternal life?" ²⁶Jesus said to him, "What is written in the law? How do you read it?" ²⁷He said in reply, "You shall love the Lord, your God, with all your heart, with all your being, with all your strength, and with all your mind, and your neighbor as yourself." ²⁸He replied to him, "You have answered correctly; do this and you will live."

continue

phasizing the sinister quality of the lawyer's question.

Jesus turns the encounter to his advantage. The law that the lawyer quotes is the Jewish Shema, the prayer a devout Jew would recite every day (Deut 6:4-5). The second half is found in Leviticus 19:18. By endorsing the lawyer's reply, Jesus proves to him and to all listeners that he and his message are not contrary to the Jewish tradition; rather, Jesus forces the audience to see his teaching as an elaboration or refinement of that tradition.

The Parable of the Good Samaritan

[29]But because he wished to justify himself, he said to Jesus, "And who is my neighbor?" [30]Jesus replied, "A man fell victim to robbers as he went down from Jerusalem to Jericho. They stripped and beat him and went off leaving him half-dead. [31]A priest happened to be going down that road, but when he saw him, he passed by on the opposite side. [32]Likewise a Levite came to the place, and when he saw him, he passed by on the opposite side. [33]But a Samaritan traveler who came upon him was moved with compassion at the sight. [34]He approached the victim, poured oil and wine over his wounds and bandaged them. Then he lifted him up on his own animal, took him to an inn and cared for him. [35]The next day he took out two silver coins and gave them to the innkeeper with the instruction, 'Take care of him. If you spend more than what I have given you, I shall repay you on my way back.' [36]Which of these three, in your opinion, was neighbor to the robbers' victim?" [37]He answered, "The one who treated him with mercy." Jesus said to him, "Go and do likewise."

continue

The scholar of the law, however, presses the point with his next question: "And who is my neighbor?" (v. 29). In this verse Luke states that the lawyer wishes to "justify himself," that is, to prove to Jesus in front of the people that he, the legal scholar, is in good stead in the eyes of God. Jesus challenges the lawyer further by responding with the parable of the Good Samaritan.

10:30-37 The parable of the Good Samaritan

Upon the death of King Solomon, Samaria, the region north of Judea, became the center of the northern kingdom at the division of the united monarchy. The Assyrians conquered it in 722 B.C., carted away most of the Israelite inhabitants, and replaced them with conquered peoples from other parts of their empire. These newcomers married into those Israelites left behind, resulting in a population too mixed for the religious Jews in the south to consider part of the covenant. In addition, these northerners, holding only to the books of Genesis through Deuteronomy, maintained their religious cult on Mount Gerizim in Shechem, whereas the Jews in the south saw true worship as taking place only in Jerusalem. The animosity was mutual, as we see in Luke 9:52-54. Samaritans still live and worship on Mount Gerizim today.

This parable exists only in Luke and reflects the theological direction set out in the Gospel and the Acts of the Apostles. The shock value of using a Samaritan as the protagonist in this parable is twofold. The road from Jerusalem to Jericho is solidly in Judea; thus the Samaritan is an unwelcome foreigner in an unfriendly country. The mention of this road also forces the audience to consider the possibility that he has worshiped in Jerusalem. Secondly, for any Samaritans who might hear this parable, this protagonist, by virtue of his journey to Jerusalem, would be a national traitor. On all fronts, then, he can claim no ethnic allegiance, and no people will claim him.

First the priest and then the Levite happen upon the half-dead victim. As officials in the Jerusalem temple, from which they are most probably returning, their prime concern is maintaining ritual purity. There has been shedding of blood, and if the man is dead, they would disqualify themselves from any temple service until undergoing the proper ritual purification, a time-consuming practice. They both avoid the problem by crossing to the other side of the road. The only one to respond mercifully is the outsider of two closed societies.

The searing lesson of this parable comes in verses 36-37. The lawyer would know from Leviticus 19:18 that a neighbor is defined as one's countryman and is limited by ethnic background. The parable, however, breaks through such an interpretation. The neighbor is the one who acts compassionately toward another, ethnic divisions notwithstanding.

Although the parable is prompted by an antagonistic question from a Jewish scholar, it would be wrong to think that this parable is addressed only to the ancient Jewish audience. In the Acts of the Apostles, Luke has an evangelizing mission to Samaria. This parable would have been as difficult for Samaritans to listen to as it would have been for the Jews. After all, the Samaritan is in Jewish territory returning from a Jewish holy city, and, depending on how one would want to view the tale, he aids a Jewish unfortunate.

The lesson for the Lukan community is the same for today's reader. To be a neighbor forces a Christian to go beyond friend and family and extend welcome and mercy to the outcast and even to one's enemy.

The **Good Samaritan** becomes a model for becoming neighbor of those in need: "Today, there is an inescapable duty to make ourselves the neighbor of every individual, without exception, and to take positive steps to help a neighbor whom we encounter, whether that neighbor be an elderly person abandoned by everyone, a foreign worker who suffers the injustice of being despised, a refugee, an illegitimate child wrongly suffering for a sin of which the child is innocent, or a starving human being who awakens our conscience by calling to mind the words of Christ: 'As you did it to one of the least of these my brothers or sisters, you did it to me' (Mt 25:40)" (*Pastoral Constitution on the Church in the Modern World*, 27).

10:38-42 The discipleship of Martha and Mary

Traditionally, many have seen this story, which appears only in Luke, as a comparison between the Christian active life, symbolized by Martha, and the contemplative life, represented by Mary. Some exegetes interpret it as Luke's subtle way of silencing and sidelining women in the Christian ministry. The Lukan

---

Martha and Mary

³⁸As they continued their journey he entered a village where a woman whose name was Martha welcomed him. ³⁹She had a sister named Mary [who] sat beside the Lord at his feet listening to him speak. ⁴⁰Martha, burdened with much serving, came to him and said, "Lord, do you not care that my sister has left me by myself to do the serving? Tell her to help me." ⁴¹The Lord said to her in reply, "Martha, Martha, you are anxious and worried about many things. ⁴²There is need of only one thing. Mary has chosen the better part and it will not be taken from her."

CHAPTER 11

The Lord's Prayer

¹He was praying in a certain place, and when he had finished, one of his disciples said to him, "Lord, teach us to pray just as John taught his disciples." ²He said to them, "When you pray, say:

continue

---

context, as others have pointed out, challenges both these assumptions.

Mary and Martha share a common ministry in the church. They are models for both men and women of a partnership in service to the reign of God. In this service the love of God is the source and end of all human endeavor, which Mary remembers but Martha seems to have forgotten. The gentle correction that Jesus offers Martha is a reminder to her that work is nothing without its connection to God. For this reason Martha needs Mary as much as Mary needs Martha.

11:1-13 Teachings on prayer

The Our Father or Lord's Prayer (11:1-4) has a revered place within the Christian tradition. With its references to the "name" (v. 2), "bread" (v. 3), and "sins" (v. 4), this prayer underscores a Jewish background. The differences between the Matthean and the Lukan accounts reflect a

Father, hallowed be your name,
 your kingdom come.
 ³Give us each day our daily bread
 ⁴and forgive us our sins
 for we ourselves forgive everyone in debt
  to us,
 and do not subject us to the final test."

Further Teachings on Prayer

⁵And he said to them, "Suppose one of you has a friend to whom he goes at midnight and says, 'Friend, lend me three loaves of bread, ⁶for a friend of mine has arrived at my house from a journey and I have nothing to offer him,' ⁷and he says in reply from within, 'Do not bother me; the door has already been locked and my children and I are already in bed. I cannot get up to give you anything.' ⁸I tell you, if he does not get up to give him the loaves because of their friendship, he will get up to give him whatever he needs because of his persistence.

The Answer to Prayer

⁹"And I tell you, ask and you will receive; seek and you will find; knock and the door will be opened to you. ¹⁰For everyone who asks, receives; and the one who seeks, finds; and to the one who knocks, the door will be opened. ¹¹What father among you would hand his son a snake when he asks for a fish? ¹²Or hand him a scorpion when he asks for an egg? ¹³If you then, who are wicked, know how to give good gifts to your children, how much more will the Father in heaven give the holy Spirit to those who ask him?"

continue

dress with Matthew's by adding the phrase "Our . . . in heaven" to "Father" in their versions of Luke's text. Luke's address here, however, matches all the other instances where the Lukan Jesus prays: "I give you praise, Father, Lord of heaven and earth" (10:21); "Father, if you are willing, take this cup away from me" (22:42); "Father, forgive them, they know not what they do" (23:34); and "Father, into your hands I commend my spirit" (23:46).

The structure is the same in the Lukan and Matthean accounts, subtle differences between the two notwithstanding. They both open by hallowing God's name, thereby affirming the divine majesty. They then move to Christ's intermediary role and conclude with a human petition.

Many see Luke's use of "sins" as his way of demonstrating Christ's efficacy. With his merciful forgiveness manifested in his passion, death, and resurrection, Jesus defeats Satan by breaking the vicious circle of suffering, fear, hate, and revenge the devil uses to hold humankind in thrall. The person at prayer asks Christ to forgive, and Christ has done so; therefore the person must also forgive.

Matthew's version of the Our Father (see Matt 6:9-13) is better known; indeed, this title for the prayer comes from Matthew's account and not from Luke's. It is Matthew's rendition that also appears to be the basis for the Our Father found in the early Christian work called the *Didache* (8:2). The *Didache*'s version of the prayer became the form used throughout the centuries and includes the doxology that many Christian churches use in their worship. With the Lord's Prayer as a background, Luke continues the teaching on prayer with the parable of the importunate friend, a reading found only in Luke. Luke's wry comparison between divine response and human reaction—"if he does not get up to give him the loaves because of their friendship, he will get up to give him whatever he needs because of his persistence"—is echoed in the Lukan parable of the persistent widow (18:1-8). The point is that if humans will act on behalf of the petitioner solely from self-serving interest, how much

different theological nuance. While Luke, for example, does not highlight the separation between heaven and earth, Matthew does so by use of such phrases as "Our Father in heaven" (6:9) and "your will be done, / on earth as in heaven" (6:10). This discrepancy led many ancient scribes to try to harmonize Luke's admore will God act from love. According to the Palestinian-Jewish custom of the day, the whole family slept on floor bedding in a single room, above the animals. To open the door would not only rouse the family but would also cause a fuss with the livestock, and all in the dark.

Luke tells us how prayers are answered (11:9-13). In his schema they have a natural, thematic, and visual flow from the parable. Someone coming at night would have to *seek* the house and door of a friend. Once found, he or she would have to *knock* at the door persistently to rouse the inhabitant to *open* it. The references to a snake and a scorpion provide insight into human response to an answered prayer. The listener or hearer would answer the rhetorical questions in verses 11-12 with a firm "None!" Such imagery, however, calls a person to faith. What might appear to be a snake or a scorpion at first glance might actually be the granted request. Again, the reader encounters Luke's analogical style based on divine response and human reaction (11:13).

The "Our Father" (the Lord's Prayer) falls almost dead center in the Sermon on the Mount. It is the central prayer of all disciples of Jesus. Just as Jews pray the Shema Israel from memory as a hallmark of their identity and faith (Deut 6:4-5; "Hear, O Israel! . . ."), so Christians pray the Our Father from memory. Although this prayer exists in two versions, in Matthew and in Luke, the Matthean version is the one that the church has prayed for centuries, most likely under the influence of consistent liturgical usage. In fact, it is always prayed in the Mass just prior to the communion rite. The chart below sets forth a comparison of the two versions. Scholars generally deem Luke's more streamlined version to be closer to the form that Jesus actually prayed. Matthew's version exhibits more liturgical influence.

Matthew's Version (6:9-15)	Luke's Version (11:2-4)
Our Father in heaven	Father
Hallowed be your name	Hallowed be your name
Your kingdom come	Your kingdom come
Your will be done on earth as in heaven	
Give us today our daily bread	Give us each day our daily bread
Forgive us our debts as we forgive our debtors	Forgive us our sins, for we forgive everyone in debt to us
Do not subject us to the test	Do not subject us to the final test
But deliver us from the evil one	

Jesus and Beelzebul

[14]He was driving out a demon [that was] mute, and when the demon had gone out, the mute person spoke and the crowds were amazed. [15]Some of them said, "By the power of Beelzebul, the prince of demons, he drives out demons." [16]Others, to test him, asked him for a sign from heaven. [17]But he knew their thoughts and said to them, "Every kingdom divided against itself will be laid waste and house will fall against house. [18]And if Satan is divided against himself, how will his kingdom stand? For you say that it is by Beelzebul that I drive out demons. [19]If I, then, drive out demons by Beelzebul, by whom do your own people drive them out? Therefore they will be your judges. [20]But if it is by the finger of God that [I] drive out demons, then the kingdom of God has come upon you. [21]When a strong man fully armed guards his palace, his possessions are safe. [22]But when one stronger than he attacks and overcomes him, he takes away the armor on which he relied and distributes the spoils. [23]Whoever is not with me is against me, and whoever does not gather with me scatters.

The Return of the Unclean Spirit

[24]"When an unclean spirit goes out of someone, it roams through arid regions searching for rest but, finding none, it says, 'I shall return to my home from which I came.' [25]But upon returning, it finds it swept clean and put in order. [26]Then it goes and brings back seven other spirits more wicked than itself who move in and dwell there, and the last condition of that person is worse than the first."

True Blessedness

[27]While he was speaking, a woman from the crowd called out and said to him, "Blessed is the womb that carried you and the breasts at which you nursed." [28]He replied, "Rather, blessed are those who hear the word of God and observe it."

continue

11:14-23 The Beelzebul controversy

Each Gospel shows some version of the Beelzebul controversy. Although much of this section is from Q, there is evidence of what is called a "Marcan-Q Overlap"; that is, Q material is intricately tied up with Marcan narrative. A comparison between Matthew 12:29, Luke 11:20-21, and Mark 3:27 is such an example. To be sure, there are no Johannine parallels to the synoptic readings here, but there are certainly traces of such accusations against Jesus at several points in the Fourth Gospel: John 7:20; 8:48-52; 10:20-21. This multiple attestation makes certain the conclusion that Jesus was accused of being in league with the devil during his ministry.

Luke uses this pericope as one of the defining moments in his two-volume narrative. Whereas Matthew and Mark both state that someone must first tie up the strong man, Luke states that someone must overcome or be victorious over the strong man (11:22). There has been evidence of victory all along in the Lukan text.

11:24-26 The return of the evil spirit

Luke sees the contest with Satan as a real battle, and the enemy does not relinquish control easily. The house to which the seven other evil spirits return is the same good one from which the unclean spirit had previously departed. Their roaming through "arid regions searching for rest" stands as a metaphor for those people who do not fill their lives with the goodness of God. Nature abhors a vacuum, and thus seven other wicked spirits find a home within the now empty individual (v. 26). This understanding can be applied to Judas, about whom Luke states that Satan "enter[s]" (22:3). Judas never allowed into his heart the grace that Jesus brings, and thus the wicked spirits take up residence there.

In Luke's Gospel, the battle between Christ and Satan, announced at the birth (1:78-79), begins at the temptation (4:1-13). Jesus has been waging and winning battles against the devil demons all along, but Christ's ultimate victory over Satan, a victory of light over darkness, will come at the cross. This theme continues in the Acts of the Apostles.

11:27-28 True blessedness

The narrative flow forms a juxtaposition of seeming opposites. After the long deliberation about Beelzebul, the strong man, and unclean spirits, a woman in the crowd turns the subject to blessedness, and does so by making a reference to Jesus' mother. Jesus' response, however, demonstrates that his call goes beyond natural kinship; indeed, natural kinship might even be an impediment (see 8:19-21).

11:29-32 The demand for a sign

Luke avoids redundancy. The narrative sequence has already informed the reader that people are testing and arguing with Jesus (see Luke 11:15), so, unlike Matthew and Mark (12:38; 8:11-12), Luke does not mention Pharisees or scribes badgering Jesus. Jesus simply continues with his teaching.

The book of Jonah forms the necessary background for any interpretation of this passage. The Lukan text in verse 30 is helpful in this regard by supplying the central element of that particular Old Testament work. That Nineveh was the ancient capital of the Assyrians, the people who ravaged the Israelite kingdom under Shalmaneser V in 722 B.C., sharpens the drama of the Jonah story. Jonah is the son of Amittai. Amittai is also the name of one of the prophets from the time of King Jeroboam II (786–746 B.C.). If the name Amittai refers to one and the same person, then it would have been understood that Jonah came from the Israelite kingdom just as the Assyrian Empire was menacing it.

Jonah is sent on a mission, therefore, into absolutely alien and hostile territory, to a land feared and despised by all his compatriots. After fits and starts, including a sojourn in the belly of a great fish (Jonah 2:1), Jonah reaches his destination and preaches judgment, with the result that the whole city of Nineveh, from the king to the lowliest beast, repents. This repentance is the sign of Jonah to which Luke refers in verses 29-30. The explanation continues.

The Demand for a Sign

²⁹While still more people gathered in the crowd, he said to them, "This generation is an evil generation; it seeks a sign, but no sign will be given it, except the sign of Jonah. ³⁰Just as Jonah became a sign to the Ninevites, so will the Son of Man be to this generation. ³¹At the judgment the queen of the south will rise with the men of this generation and she will condemn them, because she came from the ends of the earth to hear the wisdom of Solomon, and there is something greater than Solomon here. ³²At the judgment the men of Nineveh will arise with this generation and condemn it, because at the preaching of Jonah they repented, and there is something greater than Jonah here.

The Simile of Light

³³"No one who lights a lamp hides it away or places it [under a bushel basket], but on a lampstand so that those who enter might see the light.

continue

In verse 31 Luke also has a reference to "the queen of the south," or the Queen of Sheba (see 1 Kgs 10:1ff.; 2 Chr 9:1ff.; Matt 12:42). With this allusion the lesson works in reverse: the pagan makes the journey to the land of the true God. In both cases nonbelievers make acts of repentance or faith. Jesus draws a comparison and contrast between those within and those outside the pale of revelation, and in so doing, proclaims the wide invitation of God's love and salvation as well as the breadth of human response to it. In the end Jonah, with his example of the Ninevites, and the queen of the south, with her pilgrimage to Solomon, will stand in judgment of those who reject Jesus.

11:33-36 The visibility of light

These verses are a reprise of the lamp motif seen in 8:16ff. Luke elaborates the analogy here. The discourses about Jonah and the queen of the south in verses 30-31 above provide the

³⁴The lamp of the body is your eye. When your eye is sound, then your whole body is filled with light, but when it is bad, then your body is in darkness. ³⁵Take care, then, that the light in you not become darkness. ³⁶If your whole body is full of light, and no part of it is in darkness, then it will be as full of light as a lamp illuminating you with its brightness."

Denunciation of the Pharisees and Scholars of the Law

³⁷After he had spoken, a Pharisee invited him to dine at his home. He entered and reclined at table to eat. ³⁸The Pharisee was amazed to see that he did not observe the prescribed washing before the meal. ³⁹The Lord said to him, "Oh you Pharisees! Although you cleanse the outside of the cup and the dish, inside you are filled with plunder and evil. ⁴⁰You fools! Did not the maker of the outside also make the inside? ⁴¹But as to what is within, give alms, and behold, everything will be clean for you. ⁴²Woe to you Pharisees! You pay tithes of mint and of rue and of every garden herb, but you pay no attention to judgment and to love for God. These you should have done, without overlooking the others. ⁴³Woe to you Pharisees! You love the seat of honor in synagogues and greetings in marketplaces. ⁴⁴Woe to you! You are like unseen graves over which people unknowingly walk."

continue

the whole body and all human action. The way people conduct themselves determines the persons they will become. Filled with faith, these people, by their brightness, will lead others from darkness into the light of faith. The light and darkness dichotomy in this Q material is reminiscent of John's Gospel.

11:37-54 Denunciation of the legal experts

This section, called the "Woes," has a parallel in Matthew 23:1-38. Differences between the two can be seen in Matthew's concern for and knowledge of the Law, something that Luke, in writing for a Gentile audience, has no need to address.

The Pharisee literally invites Jesus to breakfast, indicated by the Greek verb *aristáō*. If Palestinian social customs of ancient times are in any way similar to those today, the breakfast would be quite substantial and would be taken around ten o'clock in the morning, but it would not be the main meal of the day, which is taken in the evening. The fact that Pharisees and scholars take issue with Jesus in the manner that they do exposes an ulterior motive: they wish to observe his behavior with hopes of gaining evidence against him. If they had really wished to honor him, they would have invited him for the evening repast. Jesus recognizes this plot and responds by revealing their true motives in front of all. He also exhibits the shallowness and hypocrisy of their deeds. Jesus' denunciation at verses 47-51 foreshadows his own death. The system that killed the prophets will also, by implication, kill him, as verses 53-54 substantiate.

It is difficult to identify which Zechariah (v. 51) Luke is referring to. Many see him as Zechariah the priest, son of Jehoiadah (see 2 Chr 24:20-22). Others have seen him as Zechariah the priest, the father of John the Baptist.

example of how "lights" and "lamps" can further evangelization. Matthew uses this Q material as well but places it at two different locations within the Sermon on the Mount (5:13-16 and 6:22-23). Luke, on the other hand, finishes this section with a wonderful simile for a true disciple. The Christian life involves

⁴⁵Then one of the scholars of the law said to him in reply, "Teacher, by saying this you are insulting us too." ⁴⁶And he said, "Woe also to you scholars of the law! You impose on people burdens hard to carry, but you yourselves do not lift one finger to touch them. ⁴⁷Woe to you! You build the memorials of the prophets whom your ancestors killed. ⁴⁸Consequently, you bear witness and give consent to the deeds of your ancestors, for they killed them and you do the building. ⁴⁹Therefore, the wisdom of God said, 'I will send to them prophets and apostles; some of them they will kill and persecute' ⁵⁰in order that this generation might be charged with the blood of all the prophets shed since the foundation of the world, ⁵¹from the blood of Abel to the blood of Zechariah who died between the altar and the temple building. Yes, I tell you, this generation will be charged with their blood! ⁵²Woe to you, scholars of the law! You have taken away the key of knowledge. You yourselves did not enter and you stopped those trying to enter." ⁵³When he left, the scribes and Pharisees began to act with hostility toward him and to interrogate him about many things, ⁵⁴for they were plotting to catch him at something he might say.

EXPLORING LESSON SIX

1. a) Why does Jesus' journey to Jerusalem receive special emphasis in Luke (9:51-53)? (See Luke 9:31.)

_____

_____

_____

   b) Why do the Samaritans refuse to receive Jesus (9:52-53)? What barriers sometimes prevent us from receiving him?

_____

_____

_____

2. Recall a time when joy filled your heart with praise for God (10:21). (See Phil 4:4; 1 Pet 1:8-9.) What role does joy play in your own faith journey?

_____

_____

_____

_____

_____

_____

3. a) How would the parable of the Good Samaritan prove challenging to both Jews and Samaritans of Jesus' time (10:29-37)? (See 9:52-56.)

_____

_____

_____

   b) Why might the parable of the Good Samaritan still be considered a challenge in some of our own communities?

_____

_____

_____

_____

4. What is the "one thing" that Jesus reminds Martha she is in need of (10:38-42)? (See 10:25-28.)

_____

_____

_____

_____

_____

5. a) What different characteristics of prayer do you see in the Lord's Prayer (11:1-4)?

_____

_____

_____

   b) What role has persistence in prayer played in your life (11:5-13)?

_____

_____

_____

6. What does Luke tell us about Mary (Jesus' mother) that also tells us that she is indeed blessed (11:27-28; 1:26-28, 39-45; 2:15-19, 51)?

_____

_____

_____

_____

_____

_____

7. What kind of sign was Jonah in Luke 11:29-32? (See Matt 16:1-4.) What does he also symbolize in Matthew 12:39-40?

_____

_____

_____

_____

_____

8. Identify some helpful practices that might provide light within one's inner self (11:33-36). (See Phil 4:8.)

_____

_____

_____

_____

_____

_____

9. What are some needs, locally or larger, which you consider worthy of almsgiving (11:37-41)?

_____

_____

_____

_____

_____

_____

CLOSING PRAYER

Prayer

"Take care, that the light in you not become darkness. If your whole body is full of light, and no part of it is in darkness, then it will be as full of light as a lamp illuminating you with its brightness." (Luke 11:35-36)

God of Light, your love and goodness and justice provide for us the light we need to follow in your Son's path and to shine as witnesses to others. Guard our hearts so that we may grow in love of you and your people. Help us to create habits that draw us into your light. We pray now for our friends and families, lifting up their needs to you, especially . . .

PRAYING WITH YOUR GROUP

Because we know that the Bible allows us to hear God's voice, prayer provides the context for our study and sharing. By speaking and listening to God and each other, the discussion often grows to more deeply bond us to one another and to God.

At *the beginning and end of each lesson* simple prayers are provided for individual use, and also may be used within the group setting. Most of the closing prayers provided with each lesson relate directly to a theme from that lesson and encourage you to pray together for people and events in your local community.

Of course, there are many ways to center ourselves in God's presence as we gather together in groups around the word of God. We provide some additional suggestions here knowing you and your group will make prayer a priority as part of your gathering. These are simply alternative ways to pray if your group would like to try something different from those prayers provided in the previous pages.

Conversational Prayer

This form of prayer allows for the group members to pray in their own words in a way that is not intimidating. The group leader begins with Step One, inviting all to focus on the presence of Christ among them. After a few moments of quiet, the group leader invites anyone in the group to voice a prayer or two of thanksgiving; once that is complete, then anyone who has personal intentions may pray in their own words for their needs; finally, the group prays for the needs of others.

A suggested process:
In your own words, speak simple and short prayers to allow time for others to add their voices.

Focus on one "step" at a time, not worrying about praying for everything in your mental list at once.

Step One	Visualize Christ. Welcome him.
	Imagine him present with you in your group.
	Allow time for some silence.
Step Two	Gratitude opens our hearts.
	Use simple words such as, "Thank you, Lord, for . . ."
Step Three	Pray for your own needs knowing that others will pray with you.
	Be specific and honest.
	Use "I" and "me" language.

Step Four   Pray for others by name, with love.
                          You may voice your agreement ("Yes, Lord").
                          End with gratitude for sharing concerns.

Praying Like Ignatius

St. Ignatius Loyola, whose life and ministry is the foundation of the Jesuit community, invites us to enter into Scripture texts in order to experience the scenes, especially scenes of the gospels or other narrative parts of Scripture. Simply put, this is a method of creatively imagining the scene, viewing it from the inside, and asking God to meet you there. Most often, this is a personal form of prayer, but in a group setting, some of its elements can be helpful if you allow time for this process.

A suggested process:

- Select a scene from the chapters in the particular lesson.
- Read that scene out loud in the group, followed by some quiet time.
- Ask group members to place themselves in the scene (as a character, or as an onlooker) so that they can imagine the emotions, responses, and thinking that may have taken place. Notice the details and the tone, and imagine the interaction with the Lord that is taking place.
- Share with the group any insights that came to you in this quiet imagining.
- Allow each person in the group to thank God for some insight and to pray about some request that may have surfaced.

Sacred Reading (or Lectio Divina)

This method of prayer invites us to "listen with the ear of the heart" as St. Benedict's rule would say. We listen to the words and the phrasing, asking God to speak to our innermost being. Again, this method of prayer is most often used in an individual setting but may also be used in an adapted way within a group.

A suggested process:

- Select a scene from the chapters in the particular lesson.
- Read the scene out loud in the group, perhaps two times.
- Ask group members to ponder a word or phrase that stands out to them.
- The group members could then simply speak the word or phrase as a kind of litany of what was meaningful for your group.
- Allow time for more silence to ponder the words that were heard, asking God to reveal to you what message you are meant to hear, how God is speaking to you.
- Follow up with spoken intentions at the close of this group time.

REFLECTING ON SCRIPTURE

Reading Scripture is an opportunity not simply to learn new information but to listen to God who loves you. Pray that the same Holy Spirit who guided the formation of Scripture will inspire you to correctly understand what you read, and empower you to make what you read a part of your life.

The inspired word of God contains layers of meaning. As you make your way through passages of Scripture, whether studying a book of the Bible or focusing on a biblical theme, you may find it helpful to ask yourself these four questions:

What does the Scripture passage say?
Read the passage slowly and reflectively. Become familiar with it. If the passage you are reading is a narrative, carefully observe the characters and the plot. Use your imagination to picture the scene or enter into it.

What does the Scripture passage mean?
Read the footnotes in your Bible and the commentary provided to help you understand what the sacred writers intended and what God wants to communicate by means of their words.

What does the Scripture passage mean to me?
Meditate on the passage. God's word is living and powerful. What is God saying to you? How does the Scripture passage apply to your life today?

What am I going to do about it?
Try to discover how God may be challenging you in this passage. An encounter with God contains a challenge to know God's will and follow it more closely in daily life. Ask the Holy Spirit to inspire not only your mind but your life with this living word.